Flexible and Focused

Critical Specialties in Treating Autism and Other Behavioral Challenges

Series Editor
Jonathan Tarbox

Flexible and Focused
Teaching Executive Function Skills to Individuals with Autism and Attention Disorders

Adel C. Najdowski
Psychology Department
Pepperdine University
Los Angeles, CA
USA

ACADEMIC PRESS

An imprint of Elsevier
elsevier.com

Academic Press is an imprint of Elsevier
125 London Wall, London EC2Y 5AS, United Kingdom
525 B Street, Suite 1800, San Diego, CA 92101-4495, United States
50 Hampshire Street, 5th Floor, Cambridge, MA 02139, United States
The Boulevard, Langford Lane, Kidlington, Oxford OX5 1GB, United Kingdom

Notices
Knowledge and best practice in this field are constantly changing. As new research and experience
broaden our understanding, changes in research methods or professional practices, may become
necessary.

Practitioners and researchers must always rely on their own experience and knowledge in evaluating
and using any information or methods described herein. In using such information or methods they
should be mindful of their own safety and the safety of others, including parties for whom they have
a professional responsibility.

To the fullest extent of the law, neither the Publisher nor the authors, contributors, or editors, assume
any liability for any injury and/or damage to persons or property as a matter of products liability,
negligence or otherwise, or from any use or operation of any methods, products, instructions, or ideas
contained in the material herein.

ISBN: 978-0-12-809833-2

British Library Cataloguing-in-Publication Data
A catalogue record for this book is available from the British Library

Library of Congress Cataloging-in-Publication Data
A catalog record for this book is available from the Library of Congress

For Information on all Academic Press publications
visit our website at https://www.elsevier.com

Working together
to grow libraries in
developing countries

www.elsevier.com • www.bookaid.org

Publisher: Nikki Levy
Acquisition Editor: Emily Ekle
Editorial Project Manager: Barbara Makinster
Production Project Manager: Stalin Viswanathan
Designer: Mark Rogers

CONTENTS

Series Foreword: Critical Specialties in Treating Autism
and Other Behavioral Challenges vii

Chapter 1 Introduction 1
1.1   How Can This Manual Help?..3
1.2   Who Can Use This Manual? 4
1.3   What Type of Learners Will Benefit From This Manual?...........4
1.4   A Consideration for Board Certified Behavior
       Analysts (BCBAs)...5
1.5   Format of This Manual...5

Chapter 2 Principles Behind the Lessons...7
2.1   Positive Reinforcement 7
2.2   Prompting and Prompt Fading...10
2.3   Chaining 15
2.4   Generalization 17
2.5   Maintenance 18
2.6   Data Collection and Graphing 20

Chapter 3 Self-Awareness, Inhibition, and Self-Management.............23
3.1   Self-Awareness..24
3.2   Self-Management...26

Chapter 4 Attention...31
4.1   Morning and Evening Routines..34
4.2   Homework Routine 36
4.3   Sustained Attention 42

Chapter 5 Organization 47
5.1   Cleaning Bedroom 48
5.2   Organizing Homework and School Supplies 50
5.3   Organizing Personal Spaces...51

Chapter 6 Problem Solving, Time Management, and Planning **57**
6.1   Problem Solving 57
6.2   Problem Solving Lesson 58
6.3   Time Management 64
6.4   Time Management Lesson 65
6.5   Planning 70
6.6   Using a Planner/Device for Planning 71
6.7   Planning: Short- and Long-Term Goals 71
6.8   Planning: Social Plans and Social Media 76

Chapter 7 Working Memory **81**
7.1   Studying Skills 82
7.2   Remembering to Turn In Homework 84
7.3   Keeping Track of Personal Items 86

Chapter 8 Emotional Self-Regulation and Flexibility **89**
8.1   Emotional Self-Regulation 90
8.2   Flexibility 94
8.3   Flexibility Lesson 95

Chapter 9 Troubleshooting **101**
9.1   Antecedent Manipulations 101
9.2   Reinforcement Procedures 102
9.3   Sufficient Learning Opportunities 102
9.4   Component Skills and Prerequisite Skills 103
9.5   Attention Deficits 103
9.6   Apps 103
9.7   Make It Fun 104

Appendix A **105**
References **107**
Index **109**

For additional information on the topics covered in the book, visit the companion web site: http://booksite.elsevier.com/9780128098332

Series Foreword: Critical Specialities in Treating Autism and Other Behavioral Challenges

PURPOSE

The purpose of this series is to provide treatment manuals that address topics of high importance to practitioners working with individuals with autism spectrum disorders (ASDs) and other behavioral challenges. This series offers targeted books that focus on particular clinical problems that have not been sufficiently covered in recent books and manuals. This series includes books that directly address clinical specialties that are simultaneously high prevalence (i.e., every practitioner faces these problems at some point) and yet are also commonly known to be a major challenge, for which most clinicians do not possess sufficient specialized training. The authors of individual books in this series are top-tier experts in their respective specialties. The books in this series will help solve the problems practitioners face by taking the very best in practical knowledge from the leading experts in each specialty and making it readily available in a consumable, practical format. The overall goal of this series is to provide useful information that clinicians can immediately put into practice.

The primary audience for this series is professionals who work in treatment and education for individuals with ASD and other behavioral challenges. These professionals include board certified behavior analysts (BCBAs), speech and language pathologists (SLPs), licensed marriage and family therapists (LMFTs), school psychologists, and special education teachers. Although not the primary audience for this series, parents and family members of individuals with ASD will find the practical information contained in this series highly useful.

Series Editor
Jonathan Tarbox, PhD, BCBA-D
FirstSteps for Kids
University of Southern California, Los Angeles, CA, United States

Dr. Jonathan Tarbox is the Program Director of the Masters of Science in Applied Behavior Analysis (ABA) program at the University of Southern California, as well as Director of Research and a Regional Clinic Director at FirstSteps for Kids. He is Associate Editor of the journal *Behavior Analysis in Practice* and serves on the editorial boards of five major scientific journals related to autism and behavior analysis. He has published 2 books on autism treatment and well over 70 peer-reviewed journal articles and chapters in scientific texts. His research focuses on behavioral interventions for teaching complex skills to individuals with autism. He is a frequent presenter at autism and ABA conferences worldwide, and a regular guest on television and radio.

Adel Najdowski, PhD, BCBA-D is an Associate Professor and Program Director of MS in Behavioral Psychology at Pepperdine University. Dr. Najdowski has provided ABA-based services to children with autism for 20 years. Between 2005 and 2010, she led the development of Skills, an online curriculum for children with autism. In 2014, Dr. Najdowski co-authored, *Evidence-Based Treatment for Children with Autism: The CARD Model*. She has over 40 publications in peer-reviewed journals, book chapters in scientific texts, and articles in popular media. Dr. Najdowski has served on the editorial boards of the *Journal of Applied Behavior Analysis* and *Behavior Analysis in Practice* and as a Guest Editor for a special issue in *Research in Autism Spectrum Disorders*. Her current research interests include teaching higher-order skills to children with autism and assessment and curriculum design for children with autism.

## CHAPTER 1

Introduction

The term *executive function* is traditionally used to refer to the "chief operating system" located in the prefrontal region of the brain, which is used to engage in cognitive processes required for goal-directed behavior. Some common executive function processes used for goal-directed behavior include working memory, task initiation, sustained attention, inhibition, flexibility, planning, organization, and problem solving. If you aren't already familiar with executive functions, it probably sounds like a complicated mess. If you're already confused, don't worry, I can honestly say that is how I felt the first time I learned about executive functions.

From a practical standpoint, the easiest way to explain executive functioning is to give you an example of what I would tell my grandmother if she asked me to explain it. Executive functions involve everything that you do every day to manage your own behavior. For example, this could involve all the behaviors it takes to make it to an appointment on time. First, you have to plan in advance by scheduling your appointment (i.e., planning). You choose a free time that is in your schedule that will still allow you to get to all your other responsibilities, including drive time and buffer time in case something goes wrong. If you need to dress a certain way for the event or will need to bring items you don't have, you will shop at least a day or two in advance for new clothes or needed items. The night before the appointment, you will think about what needs to be done and potentially get some of the tasks done that night such as filling up your gas tank with gas, ironing and laying out your clothes, packing your bag in advance (i.e., organization), and determining whether you will need to bring drinks, snacks, or a meal, and what you will bring. You will also calculate how far you have to drive and how long it will take depending on traffic, and decide by what time you should leave your house. Then, you will consider how long you will need to take a shower, eat breakfast, and gather last-minute drinks and snacks in order to leave

Flexible and Focused. DOI: http://dx.doi.org/10.1016/B978-0-12-809833-2.00001-7

the house on time. After these calculations, you will set your alarm clock so that you can get up at the time planned (i.e., time management). When the alarm goes off the next morning, you will initiate the task of getting ready to leave the house (i.e., task initiation). You will remember what needs to be done (i.e., working memory) and stay focused on relevant tasks (i.e., sustained attention) in an effort to leave the house on time. You will avoid becoming distracted by social media, phone calls, or additional activities that will deter you from getting ready on schedule (i.e., inhibition). As you start driving to the appointment, you notice that the freeway exit you are supposed to take is closed, so you decide you'll have to get off at the next exit. While you are in the car, you take a sip of coffee and spill it on your white blouse. You look at the time and realize you don't have enough time to stop somewhere to try to clean out the stain, so you decide you will wear a cardigan that you have in your car over the blouse. Then, the next opportunity you get to use the bathroom, you will try to wash out the stain (i.e., problem solving and flexibility). You arrive to your appointment with a couple of minutes to spare. You scope out the location of the bathroom and decide you'll go there when the opportunity arises.

Wow! Did you ever realize just how much self-management goes into making it to one appointment? It's no wonder that parents feel crazy when their children are young. They are not only engaging in self-management but they are also managing their children, since their children don't yet have the skills to do many things independently. Then, as children age, parents start slowly doling out some of the responsibility to their children. Many typically developing children do great with taking on the additional responsibility, yet others just can't seem to wrap their heads around self-management. Such disorganized children get easily distracted and forget what they are doing, leading their parents to nag them to complete a task such as getting ready for school. Due to their distractibility, children with executive dysfunction are often late to school and extracurricular activities. They lose their personal belongings such as sweatshirts, water bottles, and soccer balls, because they forget to bring them home when they go on an outing and they can't remember where they left them. They even lose their personal belongings at home because they don't put things away. They forget to bring home the books they will need for homework, and when they do their homework, they forget to turn it in. Their backpacks, desks, and closets look like a bomb went off and are completely unkempt. They act impulsively and do things without thinking about potential consequences. They get stuck easily when problems arise and are inflexible with solutions and let their emotions get out of control. It's exhausting thinking about what that means, not only for the parents, but also for the learner, who is receiving the brunt of disapproval from caregivers, teachers, and coaches.

1.1 HOW CAN THIS MANUAL HELP?

Although traditionally executive functions are considered brain functions, there's something you should know about me before continuing to read this book. I am not a neuroscientist; I have a doctorate in psychology and am a Board Certified Behavior Analyst (BCBA-D). Given that my background is behavior analysis, I believe that all executive functions involve behavior. For example, the brain function of memory involves someone engaging in behavior. To remember the name of a person they just met, they may rehearse the name once or twice, think of another person with the same name, or ask the person how they spell their name so that they can visualize the spelling of it. All of these are considered behaviors one engages in that get lumped into the brain function of memory. I also believe that behavior can be learned and strengthened by one's experience in one's learning history and environment. Thus, although individuals with executive function deficits may appear to have the inability to engage in the associated behaviors, I believe that if even a small portion of executive function performance is learned behavior, we should be able to improve it. My saying that executive functions involve behavior should in no way be interpreted as denying that the human brain participates. Rather, it is my way of saying that, as behavior change-agents, we should make the most of what we can do to teach behaviors that will allow individuals with executive function deficits to participate to their fullest in goal-directed behavior. There is no pill or brain surgery yet that can fix brain mechanisms that may not be working at their fullest, but there are principles and procedures of learning and motivation that are proven to help people learn. Put simply, the aim of this manual is to harness these principles and procedures to provide tools for practitioners, educators, and parents to help learners improve their executive function skills.

1.2 WHO CAN USE THIS MANUAL?

Do the examples of the chaotic behavior outlined earlier sound like your child or a learner with whom you are working? Are you interested in teaching the learner ways to engage in self-management? If so, this manual is for you! My goal in writing this manual is to provide easy-to-use lessons, data sheets, and tools (for printable tools, see the companion website to this manual) for practitioners, educators, and parents to tackle common problems observed in learners with executive function deficits.

1.3 WHAT TYPE OF LEARNERS WILL BENEFIT FROM THIS MANUAL?

This manual was written for kindergarten to adult-aged learners. I have been working with learners diagnosed with autism spectrum disorder (ASD) since 1995, so there's no question that this population is my passion and specialty. However, the principles and procedures of applied behavior analysis (ABA), which form the foundation of this manual, are equally applicable to all populations. ABA is based on principles of learning that apply to all humans and is used to change behavior in meaningful ways. For example, ABA can be used to achieve weight loss, increase physical activity, reduce smoking, increase work productivity in organizations, and improve fluency in math and reading skills, to name a few. Thus, any learner with executive function deficits can benefit from the procedures outlined in this manual. If you are unsure if the learner with whom you are involved needs this type of intervention, an assessment of executive functioning such as the *Behavior Rating Inventory of Executive Function: BRIEF* (Gioia, Isquith, Guy, & Kenworthy, 2000) should be conducted by someone qualified to administer it.

In addition to ASD, other diagnoses that are commonly associated with executive function deficits include attention deficit hyperactivity disorder, dyslexia, traumatic brain injury, and learning disabilities. Each diagnostic population has its own unique characteristics, but practically speaking, the diagnosis matters less than matching effective teaching procedures to the particular skill deficit you are trying to remediate. If you know a learner who has the types of executive dysfunction challenges discussed so far, then he or she can likely benefit from the training procedures described in this book.

1.4 A CONSIDERATION FOR BOARD CERTIFIED BEHAVIOR ANALYSTS (BCBAs)

When insurance is the funding source for ABA-based intervention, BCBAs are not able to write goals for learners that are considered "academic." Some of the lessons in this manual may appear important for the learners with whom you work, yet you may feel your hands are tied in that you are not able to target such skills. In this case, consider targeting the skills using parent training goals, and teach parents to implement relevant lessons. In addition, many of the skills described in this book directly or indirectly affect the behaviors that are the core diagnostic symptoms of ASD, so linking executive function skills to ASD symptoms can be helpful in clarifying how the treatment procedures contained in this book may be medically necessary for the learners with whom you work.

1.5 FORMAT OF THIS MANUAL

This manual was written from a practitioner's standpoint. My goal in creating this manual was to provide ready-to-implement lessons for executive functioning skills. You might have already noticed that I have written this book in casual, easy-to-read language. Just about all of the principles and procedures in this book come from experiments published in scientific journals, filled with stuffy, boring language. The "References" section and the "Additional Resources" section (Appendix A) of this book are where you can find many of these publications, and I encourage you to consult them, if you feel so inclined. In technical terms, the skills you will be teaching with the lessons in this book are based on complex intraverbals, rule-governed behavior, stimulus equivalence, and relational frame theory. For the researchers reading this book, and for anyone who may be curious, we recommend you check out the readings on these topics in the references and appendix. But for the purposes of remaining practical and consumable, the language contained in this book is intentionally down-to-earth and everyday. You might even find yourself noticing that it feels like you are talking to me, one-on-one. If that's the case, then great! For the scientists reading this book, I hope you can put your practitioner hat on long enough to appreciate the casual tone. For practitioner and parent readers, this book is specifically written to be useful to you, and I hope you enjoy it.

Chapter 2, Principles Behind the Lessons, provides the behavior analytic principles to be employed within the lessons in the remaining chapters. Chapter 3, Self-Awareness, Inhibition, and Self-Management; Chapter 4, Attention; Chapter 5, Organization; Chapter 6, Problem Solving, Time Management, and Planning; Chapter 7, Working Memory; Chapter 8, Emotional Self-Regulation and Flexibility, are organized by executive functions. The division of chapters by executive functions suggests that executive function skills may be independent of one another; however, it is actually the case that many executive function skills must be used together within the lessons that appear in the chapters. For example, when attending, one is also using inhibition by avoiding distractions and working memory when remembering the task at hand. Keep this in mind when choosing lessons to work on with learners. You may think the learner does not have issues with attention, e.g., only to realize later that attention deficits are impeding the learner from making improvements in planning skills (because the learner does not attend to the planning task). The lessons provided within the chapters include data sheets, worksheets, and visual aids that can be implemented when teaching. Finally, Chapter 9, Troubleshooting, provides ideas for troubleshooting should problems arise as you begin to implement strategies. Rest assured, problems will arise, as there is no one-size-fits-all cookie-cutter approach that will work for every learner. There is also no way that I could possibly think of all the problems that you may encounter, but it is my hope that I have at least touched upon some of the most common problems. Like all of the other work you do, the lessons in this book will need to be customized and/or extended in order to meet the individual needs of learners.

## CHAPTER 2

Principles Behind the Lessons

Several key principles need to be applied in all the lessons presented in this manual. Rather than repeating them in every chapter, they are summarized here in one place. But make sure you remember to consider all of these principles as you adapt the lessons for learners. If you're a behavior analyst, you may be able to skip most of this chapter; however, I would recommend that you read Sections 2.2 and 2.4, as I have included some nontraditional ideas in these areas.

2.1 POSITIVE REINFORCEMENT

Probably the most important thing to know about behavior is that a person is pretty much always either gaining access to something desirable or avoiding something undesirable. In other words, if there is no pay-off for engaging in the behavior, the behavior won't continue to occur. You may find this hard to believe and want to challenge this point; however, take a moment to think about it. In every single thing you do in your life, you either get something good from it or avoid something you don't like. For example, you go to work to earn money and make a difference (gain desirable consequences) and/or to avoid being homeless and failing to provide for your family (avoid undesirable consequences). You clean your house so it is enjoyable to be in (gain desirable consequence) and/or to avoid being judged by friends or making your spouse angry (avoid undesirable consequence). You take aspirin when you have a headache to feel better (gain desirable consequence) and remove the pain (avoid undesirable consequence). I could go on and on, but I will spare you more examples. If this concept seems foreign—or maybe familiar but overly simplistic—take a minute to try to think of what you do that *doesn't* result in either getting something good or avoiding something bad.

Positive reinforcement refers to the strengthening of behavior by providing access to a highly preferred item or activity contingent upon

Flexible and Focused. DOI: http://dx.doi.org/10.1016/B978-0-12-809833-2.00002-9

the behavior. Positive reinforcement is the key to increasing a desired behavior. Thus, when initially teaching skills, we start with immediate and frequent reinforcement. While providing immediate access to a tangible reinforcer (e.g., toys, activities, foods) for every independent response is certainly effective for strengthening behavior, it isn't always practical. Which responses and how often they should be reinforced will vary depending on the learner. If the learner responds well to praise, you may be able to provide praise for each step of a task and save the tangible reinforcer for when the learner finishes the whole task successfully. However, if the learner loses interest or gets frustrated easily, you may want to provide more frequent access to tangibles or breaks throughout the process. Alternatively, you may choose to set up a system that includes points or tokens that the learner would earn for each independent step. He could then use the points/tokens to buy items from a reinforcer list. In order for the points/tokens to have value associated with them, you will need to explain the system to the learner and also show him how quickly and easily he can earn access to preferred items by receiving points/tokens. In other words, make sure there are some items on the list that cost less than others and can be purchased after just a few points/tokens have been earned. This allows the learner to receive quick access to preferred items but also teaches the learner the concept of self-control and saving up to earn a bigger and more preferred reinforcer later.

Once the learner is able to exhibit the skill independently and reaches a mastery criterion, you will begin to gradually provide reinforcers intermittently. For example, instead of providing the reinforcer after each correct response, you will begin to provide the reinforcer on average every third response, and so on. The eventual goal is for the naturally occurring consequences to maintain the learner's behavior. For example, the natural consequence of putting your toys away where they belong is that you can find them later when you want them. However, some learners will never get to this point, as the naturally occurring consequences may not really serve as reinforcers for that learner. Specifically, the learner may not care about the natural consequences associated with certain behaviors such as being on time to an event or getting a good grade. For these types of learners, it is recommended that at least intermittent reinforcement remain in place to avoid the learner discontinuing to use the skills acquired. The truth of the matter is that if reinforcement is not provided at any level at all (neither contrived nor naturally occurring), the desired behaviors will eventually stop occurring, because as far as the learner is concerned, there's no pay-off for engaging in the behaviors.

2.1.1 Reinforcers Vary Across Individuals

What is reinforcing to me may not be reinforcing to you. Never assume that typical reinforcing items will act as reinforcers for any particular learner (e.g., M&Ms, stickers, praise). Rather, you should give the learner choices between two or more items or activities that he or she would like to earn. It is important that whatever items are chosen to be used as reinforcers are not provided noncontingently during other times of day, as this will decrease the learner's motivation to work toward gaining access to the items. Also keep in mind that preferences change. Thus, what is reinforcing today may not be reinforcing tomorrow or even an hour from now. So, you will want to reassess preference often when working with learners to ensure you continue to have effective reinforcers.

2.1.2 Pair Reinforcement With Praise

In general, it is recommended that you pair praise with the delivery of the reinforcer so that praise can come to function as a conditioned reinforcer. This will be especially helpful when you begin providing intermittent access to tangible reinforcers, as praise can help maintain responding. Furthermore, the learner is likely to receive praise from others in his environment, which is an example of what we hope will be a naturally occurring reinforcer.

2.1.3 Reinforcers Need to be Effective

The most important piece of information you can take away from this chapter is to remember to include a reinforcement system for every lesson in this manual. Without reinforcement, the lessons will not be effective! Reinforcers may be the natural consequence or you may need to contrive them. Keep in mind, if a lesson is ineffective, the first thing you should examine is the reinforcement system. If desired behaviors are not being strengthened, one of the following is the likely culprit: (1) the reward you are providing is not actually a reinforcer and you should reassess learner preference; (2) you are allowing free access to the reinforcer during other periods of the day, thus there is no motivation to earn it; (3) the learner is tired of the reinforcer, as it is being overused, and the learner needs to have her preference for reinforcers reassessed; (4) you are not providing the reinforcer often enough and may need to move from intermittent to continuous reinforcement; and/or (5) you are not providing the reinforcer immediately after the correct/independent response. Delays to reinforcement can decrease effectiveness.

2.2 PROMPTING AND PROMPT FADING

Prompting involves providing the learner with extra assistance to make a correct response. Hints, cues, and reminders are examples of prompts. There are many different prompts that can be used when teaching executive function skills.

2.2.1 Types of Prompts
There are a handful of traditional prompts that are used in ABA-based interventions that may be useful when teaching the skills in this book, such as, but not limited to, the following:

- *Full physical*: Providing hand-over-hand gentle guidance to complete the response
- *Partial physical*: Providing partial gentle guidance to complete the response
- *Model*: Showing the learner how to engage in the behavior
- *Gestural*: Pointing or moving eye gaze in the direction of the answer
- *Full echoic*: Providing a vocal model for the learner to repeat (e.g., you ask, "Why will you burn yourself if you touch the stove?" and then prompt, "Say, 'Because it's hot,'" and the learner repeats, "Because it's hot.")
- *Partial echoic*: Providing a piece of the vocal answer (e.g., you ask, "Why will you burn yourself if you touch the stove?" and then prompt, "Because," to which the learner says, "Because it's hot.")
- *Directive*: Directly telling the learner what to do (e.g., "Write down the steps you need to do to get ready.")

In addition to these traditional prompts, the following are additional prompts that will be helpful for teaching executive functions to learners.

2.2.1.1 Shadowing

Think of shadowing as being present with the learner and walking the learner through the task. For example, let's say you are working on teaching the learner to follow a routine such as her morning, evening, or homework routine. Initially, the parent or interventionist will need to provide shadowing to ensure the learner remains on task. Shadowing essentially involves staying with the learner throughout the task to walk her through it. Shadowing may involve using and fading out a variety of the prompts described above. For example, if the learner is being taught to sustain attention to a morning routine that involves several tasks such as washing face, brushing teeth, brushing hair, and getting dressed, shadowing would involve moving from task to task with the learner while she is completing the task and reminding her to get back on task as needed. This can be faded out by providing shadowing only at the start of each routine and then conducting check-ins every couple of minutes. For example, you might provide shadowing for the first couple of minutes of the morning routine and then leave the learner alone for a few minutes before coming back to check that the learner is still working on the morning routine. Lessons in this manual for which shadowing may be helpful include *Morning and Evening Routines, Homework Routine, Sustained Attention, Problem Solving, Organization, Time Management, Planning: Short- and Long-Term Goals, Planning: Social Plans and Social Media*, and *Studying Skills*.

2.2.1.2 Devices

Once the learner has demonstrated success with shadowing, move to using less-intrusive prompts to keep the learner on task. There are various device options that can be used for this purpose (e.g., smart phones, timers, and apps). Lessons in this manual for which devices may be necessary include *Morning and Evening Routines, Homework Routine, Sustained Attention*, and *Time Management*.

2.2.1.2.1 Countdown Beeping Timers

A countdown beeping timer can be set to indicate to the learner how much time she has to complete a task or routine. Initially, you may want to set the timer for each individual task in a routine to keep the learner on task. However, once the learner is doing well with the amount of time allotted for each individual task, the timer can be used to allow a time limit for the entire routine.

2.2.1.2.2 Countdown Visual Timers

Countdown visual timers, such as the Time Timer, display in a red color how much time is left before the timer will beep. Like the countdown beeping timer, you can either set the timer for each task or for the entire routine.

2.2.1.2.3 Interval Beeping Apps

Another option would be to set an app to beep on a predetermined interval (can be seconds or minutes) to remind the learner to get back on task. Circuit training exercise apps can be used for this purpose. The nice thing about these apps is that in addition to providing beeps on an interval for reminding learners to get back on task, they count down time and indicate when time is up. Thus, this option is similar to the countdown beeping timer but also includes a beeping sound at whatever interval you set in order to provide an auditory reminder to get back on task should the learner have deviated from the task.

2.2.1.3 Leading Questions

Leading questions can be used as prompts when you are trying to teach the learner to think his way through a task (i.e., the self-talk verbal behavior involved in prompting oneself to generate a novel response). Rather than giving the learner the answer, leading questions model for the learner the type of questions that the learner can start to ask himself covertly when engaging in tasks. These are the types of questions we all ask ourselves when we are attempting to solve problems. For example, I might ask myself, "What would happen if I tried that?" when thinking of a potential solution to a problem. Or, I might ask myself, "How long did it take me last time?" when I'm attempting to plan a schedule. If you give the learner the answer right away, you skip the chance to teach the learner this critical skill and the learner's responding can become more rote.

An example of using a leading question prompt with a learner might look like the following. Let's say you are teaching problem-solving skills. You just asked the learner to identify what might happen if he tried a particular solution, and he is not able to come up with a response on his own. You might use a leading question prompt by asking, "Well, what happened last time when you tried that?" The learner then recalls what occurred last time and is now able to answer your original question about what might happen if he tried the solution.

Lessons in this manual for which leading question prompts may be useful include *Problem Solving, Cleaning Bedroom, Organizing Homework and School Supplies, Organizing Personal Spaces, Time Management, Planning: Short- and Long-Term Goals, Planning: Social Plans and Social Media, Studying Skills, Emotional Self-Regulation,* and *Flexibility.*

2.2.1.4 Experiential Prompt

An experiential prompt allows the learner to come to the answer by having an "Aha!" moment. For example, let's say that you've already asked leading questions to help the learner state that the solution he's identified to a problem won't be effective, yet he is not catching on. You could tell him to go ahead and try the solution, or a portion of it, so that he can experience why the solution will not be effective. Then, start in again with leading questions to help identify a better solution. For example, let's say he has decided that a solution to mounting a large poster on his wall is to use tape, but you know that the kind of tape he plans to use is not strong enough to hold up the poster. You ask the leading question, "Do you think the tape will be strong to keep the poster from falling?" to which the learner answers, "Yes," so you use an experiential prompt by saying, "Let's try it and see." The learner puts the poster up, but it falls, ripping the corner of the poster. You then ask more leading questions, "So, do you still think the tape will be strong enough to keep the poster up?" to which the learner says, "No," and you ask, "What else could we try? (And let's pick something that won't rip the poster)." The learner decides that tacks might be a good solution and you agree.

Lessons in this manual for which experiential prompts may be helpful include *Problem Solving, Cleaning Bedroom, Organizing Homework and School Supplies, Organizing Personal Spaces, Studying Skills, Emotional Self-Regulation,* and *Flexibility.*

2.2.1.5 Visual Aids

Many of the lessons in this manual provide visual aids that you can use to assist the learner in acquiring new skills. The visual aids are in the form of checklists, worksheets, or task analyses to be filled out by the learner or interventionist. If you are using a visual aid, the goal is often to fade out the use of the visual aid so that the learner can complete the steps without having to consult it. There are various ways that you can do this. If the learner is filling out a checklist, you might discontinue having the learner self-monitor with checkmarks and simply hang the visual aid on a wall in a location relevant to the task/routine so that it can be consulted on an as needed basis. After time goes by and the learner continues to be successful without consulting the visual aid, it can eventually be removed.

If the learner is using a worksheet to learn planning or problem solving, once the learner is doing well with the worksheet, you could remove the worksheet and instead write key words on an index card for the learner to glance at if he forgets the steps. You could eventually work toward eliminating the index card by slowly removing steps or words from it until the index card is blank.

2.2.2 Prompt Fading

While prompts are very effective for teaching skills, learners can become prompt dependent, which means they wait for prompts rather than trying on their own. Thus, it's important to fade out prompts as much as possible, as soon as the learner is successful. When first starting to teach a skill, you will start with more assistance. Then, as the learner is able to perform the task with assistance, you will gradually remove the amount of assistance you are providing. The basic strategy for fading out most prompts is to gradually decrease the amount of help you are giving. You want to decrease it fast enough so the learner can succeed and learn quickly, but you want to fade out prompting slowly enough so that the learner does not make excessive amounts of errors, which can be frustrating and lead to challenging behavior. A good rule of thumb is to fade out prompts as fast as you can, without letting the learner make repeated errors and/or become frustrated. If the learner is making many errors and not progressing through a lesson, it is very possible that you have faded prompts too quickly.

Although ideally it would be nice if all prompts could be faded, it's not always realistic. Think about how many prompts you use for yourself to engage in self-management! You set alarms on your phone, leave sticky notes out, put items by the front door or in the car so you don't forget them, and more. As long as the learner is engaging in these types of behaviors to manage himself, it shouldn't matter that he still needs a visual to remind himself what he needs to do.

2.3 CHAINING

Chaining is a procedure you can use when you are teaching a task that is composed of many individual steps or responses. For example, brushing teeth involves many steps such as getting the toothbrush and toothpaste, putting toothpaste on the toothbrush, brushing the top, bottom, and sides of teeth, rinsing the mouth and toothbrush, and putting everything away. Many complex executive function skills also consist of chains of behaviors. For example, planning involves identifying the goal, identifying steps needed to achieve the goal, executing the steps, self-monitoring the execution, and self-correcting unsuccessful steps.

Three types of chaining procedures are commonly used: (1) forward chaining, (2) backward chaining, and (3) total task chaining. Before implementing a chaining procedure, you first need to develop a list of the steps required to engage in the task. The list of steps is called a task analysis. As you continue to read this manual, you will find that some of the lessons provide task analyses for you. However, you could also create your own task analyses, and even if you use the ones in this book, you may well need to customize them to exclude unnecessary steps or to include additional steps that are relevant to the individual learner you are teaching. Once the task analysis has been established, you can begin teaching using one of the chaining procedures.

2.3.1 Chaining Procedures
2.3.1.1 Forward Chaining
Forward chaining involves teaching the learner to initially complete only the first step of the task analysis and requiring independence of only that one step in order to earn a reinforcer. Then, once the learner is able to complete the first step independently, the second step of the task analysis is required so that the learner now has to complete both steps one and two before earning a reinforcer. This process continues in a forward fashion so that each time the learner is able to perform the required steps, another step is added on, until eventually, the learner is able to complete the entire chain (all the steps of the task analysis).

2.3.1.2 Backward Chaining
Backward chaining is the same idea as forward chaining except that you start with requiring the learner to complete the last step of the

task analysis. This means that you will perform all the preceding steps either for or with the learner and then begin to fade your prompts with the last step only. Reinforcement is provided contingent upon the last step being completed. Once the learner is able to complete the last step independently, you will require the learner to complete the last two steps before receiving a reinforcer, and so on, until the learner is able to complete the entire chain independently before receiving access to a reinforcer.

2.3.1.3 Total Task Chaining

Total task chaining involves working on all the steps with the learner from the start. You will prompt and fade prompts for steps at varying paces, depending on how quickly the learner is able to carry out various steps independently. For example, you will be able to fade prompts quicker for easier steps but may require more intrusive prompts for more difficult steps. You will have to consider how you will provide reinforcement for independent responses that occur within the chain. For example, you may provide points, tokens, praise, edibles, or whatever works for that learner.

2.3.2 Choosing a Chaining Procedure

If the task needs to be completed no matter what, e.g., in the case of a morning or homework routine, you may choose to use backward chaining. This will allow you to prompt the learner through all the initial steps and focus on the learner completing the last step prior to receiving a reinforcer.

If the task does not really need to be completed, e.g., when working on teaching problem solving, you may choose to use forward chaining and only require the learner to first identify that there is a problem. This would allow you to potentially move on to other lessons and not waste time continuing through the entire process of solving the problem. Then, once the learner is successfully identifying when there is a problem, you could move on to requiring the learner to identify that there is a problem and one potential solution before providing reinforcement. However, if you have the time to work through the problems, then perhaps you will select backward chaining instead.

Total task chaining may be good to use with learners who have the endurance to work on a task from start to finish or who learn new skills quickly. It is not necessarily a good option for learners who get frustrated with long tasks or have attention deficits and are easily distracted, and thus have difficulty with staying on task. In this case, it is recommended that you try using a forward or backward chaining procedure. The most important thing to remember is that you will need to carefully observe what is working and what isn't with each skill you are teaching to each individual learner. You may try one chaining procedure, find that it isn't working well, and then try teaching that skill with a different chaining procedure.

2.4 GENERALIZATION

Generalization is observed when learners engage in the skills we teach them in untrained but similar conditions. Generalization can be observed across stimuli, people, and settings. Generalization across stimuli is observed when the learner is able to perform the skill in the presence of a novel thing or situation. For example, if you have been teaching the learner to engage in problem solving and the learner begins to independently solve novel untrained problems, generalization across stimuli has been observed. Generalization across people refers to the learner being able to engage in the skill in the presence of individuals other than the ones who were present during training. For example, generalization across people is observed if the learner was taught to follow a morning routine in the presence of Mom and is still able to follow the routine when Mom is out of town and Dad is present. Generalization across settings refers to the learner demonstrating the skill in an untrained setting. An example would be if the learner was taught to engage in time management when at home and is now also able to engage in time management at school.

Generalization is the outcome that defines mastery. That is, a skill should not be considered mastered until generalization is observed. Otherwise, you risk the chance of the learner demonstrating rote memorization of responses rather than understanding concepts and being able to apply them in novel untrained circumstances. There are various strategies that can be implemented to program for generalization during teaching.

To program for generalization across stimuli, provide new situations and scenarios each and every time the skill is targeted in an effort to ensure that the learner is acquiring the targeted repertoire rather than memorizing responses. This procedure is called multiple exemplar training and it is the key to achieving generalization. For example, in the *Problem Solving* lesson, provide a new problem every time the lesson is targeted, and in the *Organizing Personal Spaces* lesson, have the learner organize a new space each time the lesson is targeted, and so forth. Once the learner is consistently able to respond correctly to novel untrained situations, stimulus generalization has occurred, and the learner can be said to have mastered the skill.

You can program for generalization across people by having various caregivers carry out the tasks with the learner. Train the learner's caregivers to ensure that they are not anticipating the learner's needs and doing everything for them, but are instead allowing the learner to use the skills that have been targeted during teaching when opportunities arise. For example, a child will never learn to be independent with problem solving if her parents solve all of her problems for her, without first giving her the opportunity to do it herself.

Program for generalization across settings by working on targeted skills in various settings, such as in different rooms of the learner's home, in school, and in other relevant settings. In addition to programming for generalization via contrived teaching opportunities, capture opportunities that allow the learner to continue to use newly taught skills when opportunities occur in everyday life. For example, when teaching flexibility, use every opportunity that naturally arises to teach the learner to tolerate things not going the way he thinks they should go. Do not restrict teaching to the specific contrived lessons you have planned!

The take-home point here is keep introducing new stimuli and work on teaching skills across various people and settings until generalization to new scenarios is observed. *Do not* consider a skill mastered until generalization is observed. In other words, make sure you are programming for generalization from the start, rather than merely training and hoping for generalization to happen.

2.5 MAINTENANCE

Maintenance is when the learner continues to use newly acquired skills rather than reverting back to old habits, and it is another important outcome that needs to be planned for during teaching. Like generalization, there are specific strategies you can use to make sure that newly learned skills are maintained. Ensuring the learner engages in the routines daily or at every naturally occurring opportunity will help maintain behaviors. It can be tempting during winter and summer breaks to allow practice to go by the wayside. However, keep in mind that if you choose to let newly learned skills go without practice, you will have to work that much harder to get the learner back on track when the vacation is over. Thus, it is suggested that at least some aspects of routines continue during breaks to ensure that all the hard work that went into teaching them is not wasted.

2.5.1 Training Caregivers in Maintenance

Once skills are mastered with interventionists, other daily caregivers will need to continue efforts to maintain skills. Specifically, inform the learner's parents, teachers, and other service providers about the gains being made so that everyone involved with the learner can work on implementing procedures to maintain skills. Train them on the protocols you are using and give them specific goals for how often to work on them (e.g., "work on problem solving three times per week") so that they can help the learner maintain what she has learned.

2.5.2 Thinning Reinforcement

After skills are learned, it's important to begin thinning out the reinforcement for that skill systematically. If reinforcement is simply discontinued upon mastery, it's likely the learner will stop engaging in the new skills acquired. When this happens, it's common for people who don't understand the importance of reinforcement to conclude that ABA doesn't work. It's not that ABA doesn't work, rather, it's that people don't engage in any behavior unless they are getting something good (positive reinforcement) or avoiding something bad (negative reinforcement) contingent upon the behavior. Thus, in order to ensure that the newly acquired skills are maintained, you will need to either find naturally occurring reinforcers that can maintain the behaviors or you will need to put the behaviors on an intermittent reinforcement schedule (e.g., reinforcing on average every third response).

2.5.3 Self-Monitoring Maintenance

Teaching learners to engage in self-monitoring can be helpful to facilitate maintenance of skills. For example, you could teach the learner to fill out the task analyses that are provided with the lessons in this manual. This transfers the control over to the learner and provides a visual aid to remind the learner of the steps contained in each task. You could also consider teaching the learner to graph his own data if he is motivated by visual depictions of his improvement.

2.6 DATA COLLECTION AND GRAPHING

Data collection and graphing are imperative to determine if an intervention is effective. Without data collection, you rely on your subjective interpretation of whether the intervention is effective. This can be overshadowed by one or two particularly salient events. For example, on a day when the learner exhibits a major meltdown, you may decide an intervention is not working and abandon it prematurely. Perhaps, had you collected and graphed the learner's performance, you would have identified that the behavior was improving and that the meltdown was an outlier. On the contrary, without data collection and graphing, you may continue an ineffective intervention for much longer than warranted. It's unfortunately quite common to see interventions continue for months even though they aren't working! The truth of the matter is that you should be able to observe an almost immediate improvement (at least in the amount of prompting necessary, if nothing else) within the first few sessions if the intervention is having a positive effect.

What you choose to graph depends on the important variable you want to improve upon. If the lesson includes a task analysis, you can graph the percentage of independent steps completed by the learner. If the learner needs many reminders to stay on task, you may want to graph the number of reminders required. If the learner is working on the length of time that he is able to stay on task, you may choose to graph the duration that the learner stays on task before getting distracted. Consider each skill that you are working on individually and what type of data will capture the learner's progress best. Each of the lessons in this manual provides suggestions for what behaviors to graph. See Fig. 2.1 for a sample graph sheet that can be used to track performance. You can also use Microsoft Excel or an electronic data collection software such as Catalyst, made by DataFinch Technologies.

Graph Sheet

Learner: _____ Behavior/Lesson: _____

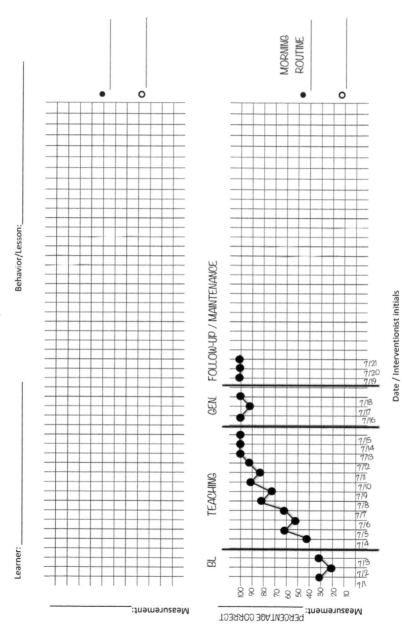

Figure 2.1 *Blank graph (top panel) and example graph (bottom panel), including baseline (BL), teaching, generalization, and follow-up/maintenance phases.*

## CHAPTER 3

Self-Awareness, Inhibition, and Self-Management

Self-awareness involves being able to take a bird's eye view of oneself and notice behaviors in which one does and does not engage, what one is good at, and what one could improve upon. People who are self-aware are presumably more successful in their relationships and careers, because they are able to see their own faults and ways in which they can improve, and they can choose to make personal goals and work on things that they are not so good at.

Learners who are not self-aware may not notice behaviors they engage in that are considered social taboos. This can potentially lead peers to feel uncomfortable around them and to socially avoid them. It can also potentially lead adults to not want their children to befriend such learners. Of course, it would be better to live in a world where people were more accepting of social differences, but often this is not the case. Thus, the learner becoming more aware of her behaviors, their social ramifications, and potential improvements that can be made to improve them, can be very important to the long-term social success of the learner. Furthermore, the parents of learners who lack self-awareness and inhibitory control often find themselves feeling frustrated, potentially leading to an increase in negative parent−child interactions.

Individuals who demonstrate inhibitory control are better at managing their behaviors. Self-management is a pivotal skill for future success in life as it involves being able to set goals for oneself to either decrease less-desired behaviors or to increase more-desired behaviors.

The following is a list of behaviors common in learners who have difficulty with self-awareness, inhibition, and self-management. If you are observing some of these behaviors in a learner, the learner will likely benefit from activities centered on teaching self-awareness and inhibitory behavior via self-management procedures.

Flexible and Focused. DOI: http://dx.doi.org/10.1016/B978-0-12-809833-2.00003-0

- is unaware of personal strengths and weaknesses
- is unaware of behaviors in which he engages that annoy others
- becomes wild or silly easily and to a greater degree than same-age peers
- acts on impulses without thinking about the consequences of behavior
- engages in maladaptive behaviors such as nail biting, skin picking, etc.
- can't seem to stop self from engaging in unwanted behaviors
- talks too loud in many situations
- has difficulty disengaging in a behavior when instructed to stop
- overengages in fidgety behaviors

This chapter provides lessons for teaching self-awareness, inhibition, and self-management. The *Self-Awareness* lesson teaches learners to notice their strengths and weaknesses and to set goals for behaviors that can be improved upon. The *Self-Management* lesson teaches learners to decrease undesired behaviors (inhibition) and increase desired behaviors.

3.1 SELF-AWARENESS

3.1.1 Procedure

1. *Self-awareness worksheet.* Start by having the learner and his parents fill out the Self-Awareness Worksheet (Fig. 3.1). This worksheet is intended to identify behaviors that the learner could improve upon by either decreasing or increasing their frequency.
2. *Identify behaviors to decrease.* Example behaviors that might need to be decreased include behaviors such as talking too loudly, biting nails, picking skin, hand flapping, licking lips, and acting wildly. Remember not to be overly judgmental when choosing behaviors. Identify behaviors that make a real difference in the social world of the learner, not just behaviors that annoy you or the parents.
3. *Identify behaviors to increase.* Example behaviors that might need to be increased include doing chores, doing homework, reading, exercising, and practicing piano.
4. *Identify how strengths can be used.* The worksheet includes questions for the learner to identify personal strengths. The purpose of these

Self-Awareness Worksheet

Name:_____   Date:_____

Directions: Answer the questions below and then come up with goals.

1. Things I am good at:_____

_____

2. Things I do that make me happy:_____

_____

3. Things I do that make my parents happy:_____

_____

4. Something I want to learn to do:_____

_____

5. Things I could improve upon:_____

_____

6. Things my parents wish I did less:_____

_____

7. Things my parents wish I did more:_____

_____

Personal goal:_____

Parent goal:_____

Figure 3.1 Self-Awareness Worksheet to be used with the Self-Awareness *lesson.*

questions is twofold. First, their inclusion adds some positivity to the exercise of filling out the worksheet. Second, the strengths of the learner can potentially be used to help the learner improve upon his weaknesses.

5. *Be positive*. Make an effort to avoid making this exercise a negative experience for the learner. Try to keep the experience as positive as possible by commenting and attending more to the learner's strengths than his weaknesses. Consider referring to something the learner cares about when discussing weaknesses. For example, nearly all superheroes have some kind of weakness and it does not mean they are bad or stupid.

6. *Identify goals*. The worksheet concludes with identification of possible goals for the learner to use to improve upon his behavior. The goals identified here can be used in the upcoming *Self-Management* lesson.

3.2 SELF-MANAGEMENT

3.2.1 Prerequisite

The *Self-Awareness* lesson in this chapter is a prerequisite to this lesson.

3.2.2 Procedure

1. *Identify target behavior*. The first step is to identify what behavior will be targeted. You can use the Self-Awareness Worksheet (Fig. 3.1) from the *Self-Awareness* lesson in this chapter to identify behaviors that the learner will self-manage. It is recommended that you start with one target behavior to avoid overwhelming the learner. Once that target behavior is tackled, you can add in more target behaviors.

2. *Take baseline data*. Collect data on the target behavior to identify how much it occurs during baseline.

   a. *Frequency*. In many cases, you will be collecting frequency of the behavior during a set observation period. Note it is important that the observation session length remain constant so that the frequency is not inadvertently inflated or deflated. Let's say, e.g., you observe 5 instances during a 10-minute observation and 15 instances during a 30-minute observation. You may incorrectly conclude that the behavior was more frequent in the second observation session, when in fact, the behavior occurred at the same rate as the first observation session (i.e., in both observations, the learner engaged in the behavior five times every 10 minutes). If you cannot always keep the duration of the observation the same, then divide the frequency by the number of minutes in the observation, to give you a mean rate per minute.

b. *Duration.* In some cases, you may also choose to record the duration of the behavior, but this is only necessary if the behavior does not have an offset that occurs soon after the onset of the behavior (e.g., more continuous behaviors such as hand flapping or exercising).

   i. *Decreasing a behavior.* If the target behavior is one that you want to decrease, an easy way to take duration data is to start and stop a stopwatch each time the target behavior occurs and ends, respectively, and then convert the total duration to the percentage of observation time the learner engaged in the target behavior. For example, if using a stopwatch to monitor hand flapping, you would start the stopwatch as soon as hand flapping occurs and then stop the stopwatch as soon as it ceases. You would repeat this throughout the observation period. Then, let's say the behavior occurred for 5 minutes during a 15-minute observation. You would divide 5 by 15 and multiply by 100 to determine that hand flapping occurred during 33% of the observation session.

   ii. *Increasing a behavior.* Record the length of the time the learner engaged in the behavior (e.g., how long she exercised, practiced piano, etc.).

c. *Take the average.* Conduct at least three baseline observation sessions and calculate the average (1) frequency of the target behavior, (2) duration, or (3) percentage of session time engaged in the target behavior.

3. *Set a goal.* In an effort to choose a goal that is achievable, you will want to set a goal that is only slightly better than the baseline average. The key to teaching the learner to decrease or increase a target behavior is to set the learner up for success so that she can access reinforcement for meeting her goal. Example goals for decreasing a behavior might be to decrease from a frequency of 10 to a frequency of 8 or to decrease from 90% of the duration of an observation session to 80% of an observation session.

4. *Identify a reinforcer.* Give the learner a choice for what she wants to earn when she meets the goal. Don't assume you already know what will be an effective reinforcer.

5. *Teach self-monitoring.* Teach the learner to self-record when she engages in the target behavior. This may begin by using shadowing (see Chapter 2, Principles Behind the Lessons, for more about shadowing), and then fading out your presence as the learner becomes more self-aware of when the behavior is occurring.
6. *Teach self-evaluation.* Communicate the goal to the learner and teach the learner to identify if she has met the goal. When the goal has been met, you might also teach the learner to engage in self-reinforcement. This would involve allowing the learner to self-deliver the reinforcer rather than requiring the learner to check in with the interventionist to earn the reinforcer. If you choose to allow the learner to use self-reinforcement, make sure to do honesty checks. Otherwise, there's the possibility that the system will fail because the learner may give herself reinforcers without actually meeting the goal.
7. *Make new goals and a terminal goal.* As the learner meets a goal, you and the learner will need to set a new goal. The idea is to make the goal gradually more difficult than the previous goal so that eventually the learner's target behavior meets a terminal goal. The terminal goal is the final goal that suggests the learner no longer needs improvement on the target behavior.

Consider mastery of decreasing or increasing a specific target behavior to have occurred once the learner meets the terminal goal for a predetermined time without prompting. An example mastery criterion is meeting the terminal goal for three consecutive weeks. In addition, consider the skill of self-management to be mastered once the learner is able to engage in self-management as outlined in this lesson independently and consistently with new target behaviors. An example mastery criterion is engaging in self-management of three new (untrained) target behaviors independently (without being asked). This mastery criterion ensures that the learner has developed a repertoire of self-awareness and self-management.

The learner can use the Self-Management Data Sheet (Fig. 3.2) to collect data on frequency or duration of the target behavior. He will use the Tracking section of the data sheet to tally frequency or duration and the Data Conversion section to calculate total frequency, duration, or percentages. You should also collect data and compare

Self-Management Data Sheet

Name:_____   Date:_____

Target behavior:			
Goal:			
Session #	**Date**	**Tracking**	**Data Conversion**
Did I meet my goal? Yes ☐ No ☐			
My reward for meeting my goal:			

Figure 3.2 Self-Management Data Sheet to be used with the Self-Management *lesson.*

your data with the learner's data in order to improve the learner's accuracy. Graph the frequency, duration, or percentage of the target behavior across observation sessions.

CHAPTER 4

Attention

Attention skills include noticing important stimuli and events when they occur in the learner's environment. Attention skills begin to develop during infancy when a baby orients his eye gaze toward his mother as she enters the room or upon hearing her voice. Around 1 year of age, learners will not only orient their attention toward unusual or interesting stimuli as they occur but they will also seek to share the moment (joint attention) with a caregiver. For example, when an airplane is flying overhead or when seeing a giraffe at the zoo for the first time, the learner will point at the relevant stimulus and make eye contact with a caregiver and then look back at the item to share the experience.

Learners with sharp attention skills are able to distinguish between stimuli that deserve attention versus stimuli that should be ignored, and they are able to disengage with less relevant stimuli to continue to attend to those that are important. For example, when completing a morning routine, as the learner sees a book lying on the counter in the bathroom, she is able to ignore the book instead of sitting down to read it and forgetting about the task of getting ready for school. This type of learner is able to inhibit getting distracted and can remember the task at hand. On the other hand, a learner with attention deficits might get distracted many times throughout the routine, requiring a parent to constantly remind the learner to get back on task. This can obviously be frustrating both for the learner who feels like his parent is nagging him and for the parent who feels like her child never listens to her.

When learners enter preschool and kindergarten, they are expected to begin engaging in tasks that take up to 10 minutes to complete. This requires engaging in sustained attention with a task without getting distracted. For example, they will be required to sit during a circle-time activity and attend to information being presented about the weather and calendar. They will be presented with worksheets and projects to complete, and as they age, the amount of time expected to

Flexible and Focused. DOI: http://dx.doi.org/10.1016/B978-0-12-809833-2.00004-2

sustain attention will increase about 10 minutes per grade level. They will be expected to attend both to tasks at school and also to complete homework at home.

As learners continue to advance in grade level, their attention skills will be tested greatly, as they will need to be able to multitask and shift their attention between stimuli. For example, they may be given a task and then stopped multiple times throughout the task to be presented with more instructions, requiring the learner to shift between working on the task and listening to instructions.

The following is a list of behaviors associated with learners who have attention deficits. If you are observing some of these deficits in a learner, the learner will likely benefit from activities centered on improving attention skills.

- has difficulty finishing tasks
- leaves little messes around the house
- forgets what he was about to do or say
- has difficult sustaining attention to an activity
- gets easily distracted during tasks
- takes much longer to complete tasks than same-age peers
- gets pulled in by unimportant details involved in tasks rather than staying focused on the overall goal
- has difficulty completing tasks with multiple steps
- has difficulty concentrating
- has difficulty staying on topic during conversation
- has difficulty shifting attention back to task once he has been distracted
- shows difficulty with doing two tasks at once such as walking and having a conversation

To improve attention skills of learners, consider working on any of the following activities:

- *Stimulus orienting.* Teach the learner to notice important stimuli as they enter the learner's environment. This should include visual and/ or auditory stimuli such as a person entering the room, giving an announcement over a loudspeaker, speaking at the front of the room, yelling "Ouch!" from across the room, loud clapping, a dog barking, an alarm going off, and so on.

- *Disengagement.* Teach the learner to disengage with unimportant stimuli with which the learner is perseverating. Let's say, e.g., that the learner has an obsession with doors and gets easily distracted when on a walk, as he wants to stop and stare at every door on every house. In this case, you would want to implement a reinforcement system for disengaging or even completely avoiding looking at doors.
- *Determining saliency.* Some learners have difficulty identifying the important stimuli that deserve attention. Teach the learner that the important stimuli are the ones that are in the center, getting all the attention from others; that are the main point or character; or that they may be bigger or in front within pictures in books, and so on. You can easily capture many of these examples in real life when you notice the learner is getting caught up with unimportant details. Teach the learner to identify the main idea of a sentence, paragraph, and eventually book and also to determine the salient activities or moments of an event such as an outing or birthday celebration.
- *Shifting attention.* Teach the learner to engage in a task and then switch his attention to a salient stimulus for a moment with the goal of being able to switch back to the original task at hand. Examples of this might be writing a book report but shifting attention to instructions or announcements being given at the front of the classroom. Another example might be when the learner is working on a task and suddenly receives a text or phone call. The learner should be able to switch back to the original task.
- *Divided attention.* Divided attention involves paying attention to multiple stimuli at once. For example, when you watch a presentation given by someone who has a slideshow, you are able to pay attention to both their spoken words and the pictures or typed words on their slides. Let's say you have a learner that is working on having conversations but he can't seem to have a conversation while on a walk or hike with someone. In this case, you would want to target walking and talking to increase the learner's divided attention between these two tasks. You could also target this skill by presenting an auditory and visual stimulus simultaneously and then immediately asking the learner to identify what was just presented. Or, have the learner watch a television show and then ask the learner to identify what the characters where talking about and what they were doing. You can also choose targets based on real-life instances in which you notice the learner is having difficulty attending to multiple stimuli presented at once.

In addition to the activities above, to help you deal with common tasks that require attention skills, the following three topics are described in greater detail below: (1) *Morning and Evening Routines*, (2) *Homework Routines*, and (3) *Sustained Attention*.

4.1 MORNING AND EVENING ROUTINES

4.1.1 Prerequisites

Make sure the learner has already mastered completing each of the tasks that will be included in the routine, such as brushing hair and teeth.

4.1.2 Procedure

1. *Materials*. Identify what tasks the learner will be required to complete in the morning versus in the evening. Use the Morning and Evening Routine Checklist (Fig. 4.1) to create a routine task list that will allow the learner to self-monitor as she completes tasks and the parents to track agreement or disagreement.
2. *Baseline*. Determine how much time the learner will be given to complete the task/routine. Base the initial amount of time allotted for each task on the length of time the learner takes to do each task during the baseline.
3. *Cuing task initiation*. Determine what will cue the learner to begin the routine. This could be an alarm clock, phone alarm, timer, or instruction.
4. *Prompts*. Determine what will keep the learner on task with completing the routine. Initially, the parent or interventionist will need to provide shadowing and/or devices to ensure the learner remains on task. See Chapter 2, Principles Behind the Lessons, for more about these prompting techniques.
5. *Chaining*. Determine whether the learner will be taught to complete the routine using forward, backward, or total task chaining. See Chapter 2, Principles Behind the Lessons, for more about chaining procedures.
6. *Reinforcement*. If using total task chaining, determine whether the learner will be provided access to a tangible reinforcer or token/point contingent upon each task in the routine or contingent upon completion of the entire routine. See Chapter 2, Principles Behind the Lessons, for more about how to develop an appropriate reinforcement system.

Morning/Afternoon/Evening Routine Checklist

Name:_____   Week of:_____

Morning Routine Alarm:_____am		Mon.		Tues.		Wed.		Thurs.		Fri.		Sat.		Sun.	
Time	Task	L	P	L	P	L	P	L	P	L	P	L	P	L	P
Afternoon Routine		L	P	L	P	L	P	L	P	L	P	L	P	L	P
Evening Routine		L	P	L	P	L	P	L	P	L	P	L	P	L	P
_____ **Earned**															
											TOTAL =			

L = Learner / **P** = Parent
Learner places a checkmark in the box once completed. Parent fills out the "P" boxes with one of the following: initials, N/A, or X

Parent initials = Parent agrees   N/A = Parent didn't require   X = Learner didn't do it

Figure 4.1 Morning and Evening Routine Checklist to be used with the Morning and Evening Routines *lesson.*

4.1.3 Mastery Criterion

Once the learner is able to self-monitor the entire routine checklist independently for a specified length of time, you can consider the skill mastered. I usually go with a mastery criterion of self-monitoring the routine for 80% of days across 1 month. At that point, I try to fade out the use of the checklist. However, keep in mind that some learners will not be able to function without the checklist, thus you may have to post the checklist so that the learner can reference it as needed. See further ideas for fading out prompts of this type in Chapter 2, Principles Behind the Lessons.

4.1.4 Data Collection and Graphing

The learner should be filling out the Morning and Evening Routine Checklist (Fig. 4.1) in the "L" (learner) column and the learner's parent should be filling out whether s/he agrees in the "P" (parent) column. Thus, both the learner and parent should both be recording data.

If you are using the Morning and Evening Routine Checklist (Fig. 4.1) to record data, graph the percentage of tasks completed each morning and evening. If the learner has more difficulty with either morning or evening, you may choose to graph them separately. If the learner takes a lot longer to finish the routine than you think it should take, you could record and graph the length of time it takes for the learner to complete the routine. If the learner requires frequent prompts to get back on task, you could record and graph the number of prompts required to complete the routine.

If you are training a parent to implement the procedures, also record and graph the percentage of tasks in the routines that the parent is monitoring on the routine checklist.

4.2 HOMEWORK ROUTINE

4.2.1 Prerequisites

Before beginning this lesson, determine if the learner's issues with homework are related to difficulty understanding the material. If it appears this is the case, seek out tutoring for the learner, as even a well-run homework routine is not going to remediate deficiencies related to the content of the homework.

4.2.2 Procedure

1. *Backpack checklist.* The first step is to ensure the learner is bringing home materials that will be needed to complete homework. The School Backpack Checklist (Fig. 4.2) can be stored in the learner's backpack and consulted each afternoon while still at school to ensure that the learner is bringing home all materials needed to complete homework. School personnel should be identified to shadow the learner through the task of packing the backpack until the learner has the hang of it.

2. *Location for completing homework.* Make sure to choose a consistent location in which the learner completes homework each day. To minimize distractions, this should be at a desk or table in a quiet area. To maximize on-task behavior, electronics should be absent during homework. This includes cell phones or devices that might distract the learner. If the learner needs to use a computer for an assignment, make sure to turn off instant messaging to eliminate interruptions by friends.

3. *Homework routine task analysis.* Once sitting in the homework location, the learner should begin the homework routine. Collect data using the Homework Routine Task Analysis (Fig. 4.3).

School Backpack Checklist

1. I need to open my homework folder or planner and look at what I have for homework tonight.
2. I need to pack:

#	Items	✓
1	Binders/Folders needed for homework	
2	Books needed for homework	
3	Other materials needed for homework	
4	Homework folder or planner	
5	Lunch box	
6	Water bottle	
7	Jacket/Sweatshirt	

Figure 4.2 School Backpack Checklist to be used with the Homework Routine *lesson.*

Homework Routine Task Analysis

Name:_____

#	Steps	Date/ Initials	Date/ Initials	Date/ Initials	Date/ Initials	Date/ Initials	Date/ Initials	Date/ Initials
1	Organizes loose papers in the backpack by placing in correct binders/folders.							
2	Identifies what needs to be done for homework (may include looking up online within school portal) and writes it on *Homework Planning Sheet*.							
3	Begins assignment 1.							
4	Checks assignment 1 for mistakes.							
5	Checks off on *Homework Planning Sheet* when assignment 1 is completed.							
6	Places completed assignment 1 in correct binder/folder.							
7	Begins assignment 2.							
8	Checks assignment 2 for mistakes.							
9	Checks off on *Homework Planning Sheet* when assignment 2 is completed.							

Figure 4.3 Homework Routine Task Analysis to be used with the Homework Routine *lesson.*

10	Places completed assignment 2 in correct binder/folder.							
11	Begins assignment 3.							
12	Checks assignment 3 for mistakes.							
13	Checks off on *Homework Planning Sheet* when assignment 3 is completed.							
14	Places completed assignment 3 in correct binder/folder.							
Percentage Independent								

Figure 4.3 (Continued)

4. *Chaining.* Determine whether the learner will be taught to complete the routine using forward, backward, or total task chaining. See Chapter 2, Principles Behind the Lessons, for more about chaining procedures.
5. *Prompts.* Determine what will keep the learner on task with completing the homework routine. Initially, the parent or interventionist will need to provide shadowing and/or devices to ensure the learner remains on task. See Chapter 2, Principles Behind the Lessons, for more about these prompting techniques.
6. *Reinforcement.* If using total task chaining, determine whether the learner will be provided access to a tangible reinforcer or token/point contingent upon each step in the routine or contingent upon completion of the entire routine. See Chapter 2, Principles Behind the Lessons, for more about how to develop an appropriate reinforcement system.

4.2.3 Homework Planning Sheet
1. Part of the routine involves having the learner write down the homework that is required. Use the Homework Planning Sheet (Fig. 4.4) for this.

Homework Planning Sheet

Name: _____ Date: _____

Homework Assignment	Estimated Time to Complete	Start Time	Completed ☑

Figure 4.4 Homework Planning Sheet to be used with the Homework Routine lesson.

2. This form has a column for the learner to estimate how long it will take to complete each assignment. Time estimation is an important skill for the learner to begin to use, as it will be very helpful for planning and time management.
3. This form also has a column for the learner to write the time that she plans to start the assignment. This is a good habit to get into, because it allows the learner to have some control over her own behavior. It is also less likely to require adult nagging to get the learner started, especially since individuals are more likely to do something they have said they will do. If the learner is not able to complete the entire routine due to difficulty with attention and getting easily distracted and off task, make sure the learner has breaks between tasks, and see the *Sustained Attention* lesson later in this chapter for working on increasing sustained attention to tasks.
4. The form purposefully does not include a column for keeping track of the actual amount of time it took to complete the assignment. It is not necessarily recommended that you use a timer to keep the learner on task, as this could add some additional pressure to the task of completing homework and lead to sloppy work or focusing too much on the passage of time instead of on completing homework. See the *Time Management* lesson in Chapter 6, Problem Solving, Time Management, and Planning, to learn more about how to teach the learner to work on a schedule.
5. If the learner does not like to write, then you can fill out the form while the learner tells you what to write.

4.2.4 Mastery Criterion
Once the learner is consistently completing the homework routine 80%–100% independently, and doing so across a variety of homework assignments you have not specifically trained her on, you can consider the skill mastered. At that point, try to fade out the use of the task analysis. However, keep in mind that some learners will not be able to function without the checklist, thus you may have to post the checklist so that the learner can reference it as needed. See further ideas for fading out prompts of this type in Chapter 2, Principles Behind the Lessons.

4.2.5 Data Collection and Graphing
For some learners, it may be helpful to have them self-monitor their completion of steps using the Homework Routine Task Analysis

(Fig. 4.3). In this case, the learner will record data. However, should you choose not to use self-monitoring, then the interventionist will record data.

If you are using the Homework Routine Task Analysis (Fig. 4.3), record and graph the percentage of independent steps completed by the learner. If the learner is working on sitting for longer intervals, you could record and graph the length of time the learner can sit to work on homework before needing a break; see the Sustained Attention Data Sheet (Fig. 4.5) in the *Sustained Attention* lesson later in this chapter to capture this. If the learner takes a lot longer to finish homework than you think it should take, you could record and graph the length of time it takes for the learner to complete the homework routine. If the learner requires frequent prompts to get on task, you could record and graph the number of prompts required to complete the routine.

4.2.6 Long-Term School Projects

See the *Planning: Short- and Long-Term Goals* lesson in Chapter 6, Problem Solving, Time Management, and Planning, for teaching the learner to make plans for completing school projects that are not due for a couple of weeks or more.

4.3 SUSTAINED ATTENTION

4.3.1 Procedure

1. *Target behaviors.* Start by identifying the skill areas in which the learner has difficulty sustaining attention. Possible target behaviors include morning and evening routines (see lesson in this chapter), homework routine (see lesson in this chapter), practicing sports or musical instruments, puzzles, constructive play activities (Legos, making a model car), and projects of any kind; also see the *Planning: Short- and Long-Term Goals* lesson in Chapter 6, Problem Solving, Time Management, and Planning.
2. *Baseline.* For the target behaviors of interest, collect baseline data on how many minutes the learner is able to stay on task without getting distracted or engaging in challenging behavior. Use the Sustained Attention Data Sheet (Fig. 4.5) to track your data.
3. *Target time length.* In an effort to ensure the learner is successful, set the initial target time length just below the baseline time length.

Sustained Attention Data Sheet

Name: _____

Task	Date										
	Time										
	Length										
	+ / -										

Task	Date										
	Time										
	Length										
	+ / -										

Task	Date										
	Time										
	Length										
	+ / -										

Task	Date										
	Time										
	Length										
	+ / -										

Figure 4.5 Sustained Attention Data Sheet to be used with the Sustained Attention lesson.

To determine your goal time length, keep in mind that a kindergartner and first grader should be expected to stay on task for 10 minutes, a second grader for 20 minutes, and increase by 10 minutes for each grade level. By high school, learners should be able to attend to a task for a couple hours.

4. *Prompting.*
   a. If the learner requires prompting to get back on task during the interval, the interval is likely too long. Start with an interval that the learner can successfully carryout on his own, even if only for a few seconds.
   b. As the learner is successful, you will begin to increase the interval across sessions. Once the learner is up to an interval that is a few minutes or longer, if you feel you must provide a prompt to get back on task, I suggest using nonvocal prompts such as a point in the direction of the task.
   c. You might also consider setting a device prompt such as an app to beep on an interval to remind the learner to "check in" with himself to determine if he is on task. See Chapter 2, Principles Behind the Lessons, for more on device prompts.

5. *Reinforcement.*
   a. When the learner meets the target time length without getting distracted or engaging in challenging behavior, provide immediate reinforcement.
   b. After two to three consecutive instances of meeting the target time length, increase the time length required to stay on task by small increments initially (e.g., 1−2 minutes or even just a few seconds if needed). This is how reinforcement will be gradually thinned out.
   c. After two to three consecutive instances of failing to meet the target time length, back-step to a previously successful time length, and then increase by a smaller increment when the learner again meets the target time length two to three consecutive times.
   d. You may need to implement different time goals for each type of task, as some tasks will be more difficult to pay attention to than others.

4.3.2 Mastery Criterion
At each target interval, you may set a mastery criterion of being able to sustain attention for two to three consecutive intervals before

moving to the next interval. Continue in this manner until the learner is able to sustain attention for the terminal interval length across various types of tasks including novel tasks.

4.3.3 Data Collection and Graphing
If you are using the Sustained Attention Data Sheet (Fig. 4.5), graph the number of minutes the learner was able to sustain attention.

4.3.4 Troubleshooting
If the learner does not even sustain attention to preferred activities, try increasing attention to those activities first. Furthermore, if the learner is having difficulty attending for even a few seconds, you may find that you first need to shape other attending skills such as eye contact, tracking, and orienting toward stimuli. For a manual on teaching these types of more basic skills, see the behavioral intervention manual written by Maurice, Green, and Luce (1996).

## CHAPTER 5

Organization

Teaching learners to be organized is something that can begin when they are young. For example, toddlers can be taught to put their toys away before getting out new toys. They respond particularly well to being taught this if you sing a "clean-up song" while cleaning (e.g., "Clean up, clean up! Everybody everywhere, clean up, clean up. Everybody, do your share!"). Placing pictures and labels on bins and drawers can also be helpful for reminding learners where things go.

Parents can come up with organizational schemes that their young children are expected to start following early. For example, by having a hamper in the learner's bedroom, parents can to teach their children to place dirty clothes in the hamper instead of on the floor. Having a location for the school backpack to be hung or for shoes and jackets to be placed right when learners walk in the front door can be beneficial. Requiring the learner to put items that belong in the bedroom each evening before bed can be enacted as part of the learner's evening routine. Chores that are related to remaining organized will also instill organization skills. These can include teaching the learner to put clean clothes away in drawers or the closet, cleaning her bedroom, and organizing her desk, closet, or dresser. Being consistent is always important when teaching learners with attention and executive function challenges, but it is especially so when teaching organizational skills. Simply setting organizational routines and having the learner stick to them every day will go a long way toward helping her establish organizational skills herself.

The following is a list of challenges often displayed by learners who have organizational deficits. If you are observing some of these deficits in a learner, she will likely benefit from activities centered on improving organizational skills.

- Has difficulty finding personal items at home
- Can't seem to find completed homework when it's time to turn it in
- Doesn't know where to put things when it's time to clean up

Flexible and Focused. DOI: http://dx.doi.org/10.1016/B978-0-12-809833-2.00005-4

- Can't seem to part with old and unnecessary items
- Items are scattered throughout school backpack and desk with no particular rhyme or reason

In this chapter, the following lessons are provided for teaching organizational skills: (1) *Cleaning the Bedroom*, (2) *Organizing Homework and School Supplies, and* (3) *Organizing Personal Spaces.*

5.1 CLEANING BEDROOM

5.1.1 Procedure

1. *Organizational scheme.* The first step is to come up with an organizational scheme for the bedroom. This involves making sure that the items that are in the bedroom have locations in which they are expected to be kept and that these locations are obvious to the learner. You can post labels or photos as needed. For example, you may choose to put labels on drawers, bins, and shelves that indicate what is stored in the respective locations. Furthermore, you may post photos next to the desk and closet indicating what a clean desk and closet look like.
2. *Task analysis.* Once the organizational scheme is indicated, use the Cleaning Bedroom Task Analysis (Fig. 5.1) to teach the learner to clean her bedroom independently.
3. *Chaining.* Determine whether the learner will be taught to complete the routine using forward, backward, or total task chaining. See Chapter 2, Principles Behind the Lessons, for more about chaining procedures.
4. *Prompts.* Determine what will keep the learner on task with cleaning her bedroom. Initially, the parent or interventionist will need to provide shadowing and/or devices to ensure the learner remains on task. See Chapter 2, Principles Behind the Lessons, for more about these prompting techniques. You can also teach the learner to fill out the task analysis himself so that he can self-monitor completion of the task.
5. *Reinforcement.* If using total task chaining, determine whether the learner will be provided access to a tangible reinforcer or token/point contingent upon each task in the routine or contingent upon completion of the entire routine. See Chapter 2, Principles Behind the Lessons, for more about how to develop an appropriate reinforcement system.

Cleaning Bedroom Task Analysis

Name:_____

#	Steps	Date/ Initials	Date/ Initials	Date/ Initials	Date/ Initials	Date/ Initials	Date/ Initials	Date/ Initials
1	Pick up items on the floor and put away.							
2	Make bed.							
3	Put away items on top of desk.							
4	Put away items on top of nightstand.							
5	Put away items on top of dresser.							
6	Organize bookshelf.							
7	Close closet door.							
8	Take out trash.							
9	Other:							
10	Other:							
11	Other:							
	Percentage Independent							

Figure 5.1 Cleaning Bedroom Task Analysis to be used with the Cleaning Bedroom *lesson.*

5.1.2 Mastery Criterion

Once the learner is able to clean her bedroom 100% independently across several days, you can consider the skill mastered. If the learner is using the task analysis to self-monitor her behavior of cleaning her bedroom, you can still consider the skill mastered but you may want to try to fade it out. However, keep in mind that some learners will not be able to function without the task analysis or some other visual aid. Thus, you may choose to post the task analysis indefinitely so that the learner can reference it as needed. See further ideas for fading out prompts of this type in Chapter 2, Principles Behind the Lessons.

5.1.3 Data Collection and Graphing

For some learners, it may be helpful to have them self-monitor their completion of steps using the Cleaning Bedroom Task Analysis (Fig. 5.1). In this case, the learner will record data. However, should you choose not to use self-monitoring, then the interventionist will record data.

If you are using the Cleaning Bedroom Task Analysis (Fig. 5.1) to record data, graph the percentage of steps completed independently. If the learner takes a lot longer to clean her bedroom than you think it should take, you could graph the length of time it takes. If the learner requires frequent prompts to get on task, you could graph the number of prompts required for the learner to clean her bedroom.

5.2 ORGANIZING HOMEWORK AND SCHOOL SUPPLIES

Use the steps below to teach the student to organize his schoolwork, backpack, and desk. Once organized, help the learner stay organized. See the *Homework Routine* lesson in Chapter 4, Attention, for how this can be built into the daily routine.

5.2.1 Organizational Scheme for Schoolwork

Kindergarten through second or third grade. This grade level usually involves a simple homework folder with pockets, wherein one side contains papers to go home (e.g., field trip forms and communications from the teacher to the parent), and the other side contains papers to go to school (e.g., homework assignments, signed forms from parent to teacher).

Starting around fourth or fifth grade. At this time, homework is better organized by subject, as students start using binders to organize schoolwork. Discuss with the learner a plan for organizing school papers.

1. Determine how many subjects the learner needs to organize.
2. Determine if papers for each subject will be organized using binders, folders, or both. Consider using binders or folders that are different colors so that each subject is color-coded. If the learner is in fourth or fifth grade, it may be possible to use one binder with dividers for each subject and then have a separate pocket folder that is organized like the homework folder described above for the younger student, wherein one side of the folder houses papers to go home (notes to parents) and another side contains papers to go to school (completed homework). If the learner is in middle or high school, the

organizational scheme will likely include several binders and folders. Either way, it's important to determine with the learner where completed homework will be placed so that it gets turned in on time.

5.2.2 Organizational Scheme for Backpack

1. *Pockets.* A backpack that includes pockets for organizational purposes is most helpful. In addition to the usual large and small pocket, a backpack that contains a place to hold the learner's water bottle is essential and a built-in change pocket to hold money is useful for learners who lose their lunch money.
2. *Small items.* If the learner has many loose items in the small pocket (e.g., pencils, crayons, markers, erasers), determine with the learner what can be kept in his classroom desk at school and what needs to be in the backpack. Then, identify whether a pencil pouch or other types of containers might be beneficial for storing smaller items.
3. *Packing backpack.* Teach the learner how to pack his backpack.
4. *Visual aid.* Take a picture of the correctly packed backpack, and place it in an agreed-upon location in the backpack so that the learner can consult the picture as needed.

5.2.3 Organizational Scheme for Desk

1. *School desk.* Determine where items will be stored in the school desk. Books can be stacked from largest to smallest on one side and smaller items stored in a pencil box.
2. *Home desk.* In the home desk, determine what will go in each drawer and on top of the desk. Smaller items can be stored in a drawer organizer or in a desktop organizer/caddy.
3. *Visual aid.* Take a picture of the learner's desk and display it on or near the desk to remind the learner where items belong in and on the desk.

5.3 ORGANIZING PERSONAL SPACES

5.3.1 Procedure

1. *Explain how to sort items.* Start by teaching the learner that there are five decisions that will need to be made regarding the items in the space.
   a. *Throw away*: Items that are considered trash will be placed in garbage bags.
   b. *Donate*: Items that someone else may want will be placed in a garbage bag or box for donating.

c. *Put in storage*: Items that the learner is not willing to donate but doesn't need or want displayed in his room (e.g., memorabilia, sentimental items from early childhood) will be placed in boxes, tubs, or garbage bags to be placed in a storage location such as the garage or attic.

d. *Goes in a different room*: Items that do not belong in the learner's bedroom will be placed in a container to be moved after sorting all of the items in the learner's bedroom. This strategy is recommended in lieu of having the learner walk back-and-forth between rooms placing items one at a time (this can be very time consuming, especially in a two-story house).

e. *Keep*: Items that will continue to belong in the learner's bedroom should be sorted. For example, as the learner is removing items from the closet, he can sort video games into a bin, place books into a pile or directly onto a bookshelf, place board games into a stack or directly onto a shelf, move shoes to the shoe location, and so forth.

2. *Negotiate items to keep versus purge.* If the learner is a "pack rat," it may be difficult to get the learner to agree to donate or place items in storage. In these cases, you will help the learner identify what is important to keep by asking, "Will you ever use it?" If the answer is, "No," then ask the learner why he wants to keep it. If it won't be used but has sentimental value, then perhaps the item is worth keeping. However, if it isn't relevant or displayable, encourage the learner to place the item in storage.

3. *Determine how much of the project to bite off.* If the learner's bedroom is extremely messy, start by working on only one project at a time. For example, start by cleaning out the learner's closet today, then work on the space under the bed next time, and so on.

4. *Use household cleaners.* Once the items are sorted, teach the learner to use the wood cleaner and rag or glass cleaner and paper towels to clean the surface of the area that was just cleared out.

5. *Find homes for items in the room.* Teach the learner how to decide where to place items that he has decided to keep, such as on closet or book shelves, under his bed, in bins, and so on.

6. *Move items that go in different rooms.* Finally, finish up by having the learner move the trash bags, donation items, storage items, and items that go into different rooms out of his bedroom and into the appropriate locations. See the Organizing Personal Spaces Task Analysis (Fig. 5.2) for a step-by-step procedure for teaching this skill.

Organizing Personal Spaces Task Analysis

Name:_____

#	Steps	Date & Area Organizing	Date & Area Organizing	Date & Area Organizing	Date & Area Organizing	Date & Area Organizing
Obtains:						
1	Garbage bags					
2	Boxes/Tubs for storage					
3	Boxes/Tubs for items that go in different rooms					
4	Wood cleaner					
5	Glass cleaner					
6	Paper towels					
7	Dusting rag					
Sorts items into:						
1	Throw away					
2	Donate					
3	Put in storage					
4	Goes in different room					
5	Keep: Sorts items being kept into piles by category					
Wipes cleared out storage area clean with wood/glass cleaner.						
1	Area:					
2	Area:					
3	Area:					

Figure 5.2 Organizing Personal Spaces Task Analysis to be used with the Organizing Personal Spaces *lesson.*

4	Area:						
5	Area:						
Determines where (closet shelves, bookshelf, under bed) and how (in bins, stacked, etc.) kept items will be stored.							
1	Items:						
2	Items:						
3	Items:						
4	Items:						
5	Items:						
Moves:							
1	Trash to garbage can.						
2	Donation items to preferred location.						
3	Storage containers to storage area.						
4	Items that go into different rooms to correct location.						
Percentage Independent							

Figure 5.2 (Continued)

7. *Prompts.* Initially, you will likely be shadowing the learner and walking him through the process of organizing his personal spaces. However, once he has organized one personal space, e.g., his closet, you should try to back off to allow him to use the task analysis on his own to work through the process of organizing an additional space such as his desk. The goal is to slowly fade out your prompts until he is able to organize a new space using just the task analysis.

5.3.2 Mastery Criterion

Consider the skill of organizing personal spaces to be mastered once the learner is able to organize novel untrained spaces consistently. An example mastery criterion could be organizing three consecutive spaces independently across three days. At that point, try to fade out the use of the task analysis. However, keep in mind that some learners will not be able to function without it, thus you may have to post the task analysis so that the learner can reference it as needed. See further ideas for fading out prompts of this type in Chapter 2, Principles Behind the Lessons.

5.3.3 Data Collection and Graphing

It may be helpful to have some learners self-monitor their completion of steps using the task analysis. In this case, the learner will record data. However, should you choose not to use self-monitoring, the intervention-ist will record data. If you are using the Organizing Personal Spaces Task Analysis (Fig. 5.2), record and graph the percentage of steps the learner completes independently.

5.3.4 Troubleshooting

You may need to start with a smaller area to organize if it's too much to organize the entire desk. If the learner feels overwhelmed or unable to attend long enough to organize a personal space from start to finish, consider breaking the personal space down into more than one organizational task. For example, instead of planning to organize the learner's entire desk, choose to work on only two drawers today and save the rest for tomorrow. Other options include providing more frequent breaks while working on the task and having the learner complete an organizational task frequently so that the mess does not become large enough for the task to be overwhelming. Finally, consider requiring the learner to complete organizational tasks before doing a preferred activity, e.g., tidying her room or desk before playing video games.

## CHAPTER 6

Problem Solving, Time Management, and Planning

6.1 PROBLEM SOLVING

According to Skinner (1974), a problem is a situation wherein an outcome would be reinforcing if one had a behavior needed to produce the outcome. Therefore, problem solving can be considered a skill that one uses to determine the behaviors most likely to result in the desired outcome. In other words, problem solving involves figuring out what to do to get what one wants.

Problem-solving skills develop around the age of 6 years and involve a complex chain of behaviors. The first step is identifying the problem. Then, the learner must identify possible solutions to the problem. It's also helpful if the learner identifies the likely outcomes of each possible solution so that the solution with the most promising outcome can be selected. Once a solution is identified, the learner must carry out the solution. If the solution is ineffective, the learner must go back to the drawing board and either select a different solution or possibly think of an additional new solution based on the information learned from the failure. In this case, the learner must demonstrate perseverance and continue to implement solutions until the problem is solved. After the problem is solved, it can be helpful for the learner to reflect on what was learned from the process by identifying what was and was not effective and how the problem would be approached next time.

There are obviously many different types of problems, some of which are nonsocial, such as not being able to get the lid off a jar and trying to figure out how to open a heavily taped package. Social problems and conflicts tend to be more complex and generally require an additional repertoire called perspective taking. This repertoire involves considering the thoughts and emotions of others within particular

Flexible and Focused. DOI: http://dx.doi.org/10.1016/B978-0-12-809833-2.00006-6

problem situations and considering possible solutions on the basis of these inferred thoughts and emotions. Specifically, prior to identifying possible solutions, the learner will need to consider what happened from the learner's perspective and then perform this same exercise from the perspective of the other person(s) involved in the social conflict. Moreover, the learner will need to consider how the possible solutions will further affect the thoughts and emotions of the parties involved.

The following is a list of challenges often displayed by learners who have difficulty solving problems. If you are observing some of these deficits in a learner, the learner will likely benefit from the upcoming *Problem Solving* lesson:

- gets into personal conflicts with others
- is always asking others for help
- tries the same solution over and over again, rather than coming up with new ideas
- gets stuck easily when doing projects
- does not appear to learn from mistakes

6.2 PROBLEM SOLVING LESSON

6.2.1 Procedure

1. *Materials.* Present a problem scenario to the learner orally, via video, or in vivo when problems arise. See the Examples of Problems and Solutions (Table 6.1) for some ideas for nonsocial and social problems.
2. *Prompts.*
   a. *Use shadowing.* Initially, use shadowing (see Chapter 2, Principles Behind the Lessons, for more about shadowing) to walk the learner through the steps of solving the problem. In doing so, you can either follow the steps outlined in the Problem Solving Task Analysis (Fig. 6.1) and present the questions in that task analysis orally to the learner, or you can use the Problem Solving Worksheets (Figs. 6.2 and 6.3), which provide written questions to which the learner should write answers (you can write them if the learner does not like to write).

Table 6.1 Examples of Problems and Solutions

Nonsocial Problems	Solutions
Need to open a package but don't have scissors	Use keys
	Rip tape off
	Tear the package open
Need a pen but can't find one	Use a marker
	Use a make-up pencil
	Use a colored pencil
Gets lost	Use GPS on cell phone
	Ask someone for directions
	Call parents for directions
Can't find cell phone	Retrace steps
	Look in the most likely places
	Ask to borrow someone's phone to call it
Zipper on pants broke at school	Tie a sweatshirt around waist
	Fasten with a safety pin
	Change into gym clothes
Forgot lunch money	Ask cafeteria workers for an IOU
	Borrow money from a friend
	Eat the snack in the backpack for lunch
Social Problems	**Solutions**
Disagreement about who gets to go first in a game	Rock Paper Scissors
	Pick a number between 1 and 10
	Let the other person go first
Disagreement about what activity to engage in during a play-date	Take turns picking activities
	Choose an activity both want to do
	Flip a coin
Getting left out of the group	Find someone else to hang out with
	Present something interesting that the group will want to do
	Ask them nicely if they'll include you
Teasing	Laugh it off by making fun of self
	Tease back
	Pay no attention
Accidentally hurt a friend	Say sorry
	Ask if they are okay
	Offer to get ice
Accidentally broke a friend's preferred item	Offer to buy a new one
	Offer the friend your own item
	Offer to fix it

Problem-Solving Task Analysis

Name:_____

#	Steps	Questions (initial prompts)	Date/ Initials	Date/ Initials	Date/ Initials	Date/ Initials	Date/ Initials
1	Identifies the problem.	"What is the problem?"					
2	Identifies own perspective of what happened. (Only use this step for social problems).	"What do you think happened?"					
3	Identifies what the other person thinks happened. (Only use this step for social problems).	"What does (person) think happened?"					
4	Identifies possible solution 1.	"What's one thing you could do to fix the problem?"					
5	Identifies likely outcome of solution 1.	"What might happen if you do (solution 1)?					
6	Identifies possible solution 2.	"What's another thing you could do to fix the problem?"					
7	Identifies likely outcome of solution 2.	"What might happen if you do (solution 2)?"					
8	Identifies possible solution 3.	"What's another thing you could do to fix the problem?"					
9	Identifies likely outcome of solution 3.	"What might happen if you do (solution 3)?"					
10	Selects the best solution.	"Which one is the best?"					
11	Implements the selected solution.	"Try it."					
12	Evaluates whether solution worked.	"Did it work?"					
13	If didn't work, tries another solution.	"What could you do differently? What could you try instead?"					
14	If worked, identifies what was learned.	"What did you learn from this problem?"					
		Percentage Independent					

Figure 6.1 Problem-Solving Task Analysis to be used with the Problem Solving *lesson.*

Problem-Solving Worksheet (Nonsocial Problems)

Name:_____   Date:_____

What's the problem?

Things I could do to fix the problem (solutions): 1. _____ 2. _____ 3. _____	What might happen if I try the solutions: 1. _____ 2. _____ 3. _____

Best Solution:

TRY IT!!! ☐   Did it work? ☐Yes ☐No
If it didn't work, keep trying new solutions until one works.

The solution that worked was:

What did I learn from solving the problem?

Figure 6.2 Problem-Solving Worksheet (Nonsocial Problems) to be used with the Problem Solving *lesson.*

 b. *Use less intrusive prompts.* Prompt correct answers to the questions using less intrusive prompts first. Less intrusive prompts for teaching problem solving include leading questions and experiential prompts. See Chapter 2, Principles Behind the Lessons, for more information about these types of prompts.

Social Problem-Solving Worksheet

Name:_____   Date:_____

What's the problem?	
What do I think happened?	What does the other person think happened?
Things I could do to fix the problem (solutions): 1. _____ 2. _____ 3. _____	What might happen if I try the solutions: 1. _____ 2. _____ 3. _____
Best Solution:	

TRY IT!!! ☐   Did it work? ☐Yes ☐No

If it didn't work, keep trying new solutions until one works.

The solution that worked was:
What did I learn from solving the problem?

Figure 6.3 Social Problem-Solving Worksheet to be used with the Problem Solving *lesson.*

c. *Fade prompts.* If you are presenting the questions vocally to the learner, as the learner is successful, begin to fade out the use of the questions that are in the task analysis. If you are using the worksheet with the learner, you will need to fade out the use of the worksheet so that the learner can complete the steps without having to consult the worksheet. To do this, you could write the following key words on an index card: (1) Problem, (2) Possible solutions, (3) Choose and try one, (4) Keep trying.

3. *Task initiation.* Require the learner to continue to work on the problem until a successful solution is accomplished.

6.2.2 Mastery Criterion

Consider the skill of solving problems to be mastered once the learner is able to solve novel untrained problems consistently. An example mastery criterion could be solving three consecutive novel problems across three days independently.

6.2.3 Data Collection and Graphing

If you are using the Problem-Solving Task Analysis (Fig. 6.1), graph the percentage of steps the learner was able to complete independently. If you are using one of the Problem Solving Worksheets (Figs. 6.2 and 6.3), you may choose to grade it afterward for percentage of independence, in which case, you will still graph percentage of independent steps completed.

6.2.4 Troubleshooting

If the learner feels overwhelmed or unable to attend to solving a problem from start to finish, try using a forward chaining procedure (see Chapter 2, Principles Behind the Lessons, for more information on chaining procedures). It might also help to choose problems that are not likely to evoke frustration or challenging behavior. For example, avoid choosing problems that might result in the learner having a tantrum. Once the learner gets the hang of solving such problems, you can then start to introduce problems that are more likely to evoke frustration. Another general tip is to start teaching problem solving with problems that have a strong reinforcer as the natural consequence for solving the problem. For example, you could secretly take the batteries out of a favorite toy to teach the skill of solving the problem of the toy not working. The natural consequence of solving this problem is being able to play with a favorite toy.

Once you start working on problems that are more serious in nature for the learner, if you notice that the learner becomes emotionally charged, see the *Emotional Self-Regulation* lesson in Chapter 8, Emotional Self-Regulation and Flexibility, for teaching the learner strategies for coping with difficult emotions.

6.3 TIME MANAGEMENT

Time management involves (1) scheduling activities based upon a predicted amount of time that the activity will take; (2) checking in with the time now and then to ensure one is on schedule; and (3) either speeding up to remain on time or readjusting the schedule as needed, in order to be on time for upcoming obligations in the schedule. Individuals who are unskilled at time management often show up late for obligations or overextend themselves when scheduling activities. They may be able to predict how long activities should take but don't provide themselves with buffer time that may be needed if something unexpected comes up (e.g., the phone rings, they can't find an item needed, they spill milk, etc.).

Even before learners are able to tell time, their parents can begin teaching them the concept of time. For example, when learners are engaged in preferred activities, parents might give warnings that count down the number of minutes before a transition will occur (e.g., "You can play at the park for 5 more minutes"). Parents may also push their child along in the morning to finish morning routines by saying things like, "If we don't leave in 5 minutes, we are going to be late."

However, it is not until learners are able to tell time that they can truly learn time management. Thus, it's important to ensure that the learner already knows how to tell time and calculate the passage of time before formally working on teaching time management. In typical child development, learners between 11 and 14 years of age engage in time management behaviors by estimating the time length of activities and adjusting their schedules. It is also in these years that learners will plan homework, after-school activities with friends, extracurricular activities, and responsibilities, such as chores.

The following is a list of behaviors often displayed by learners who have difficulty with time management. If you are observing some of these deficits in a learner, the learner will likely benefit from the upcoming *Time Management* lesson:

- is often late for commitments
- overextends self with commitments
- fails to end tasks with enough time to transition to the next task scheduled
- does not consider how long tasks will take when scheduling self
- does not get tasks done within allotted time
- gets off task and starts working on other things

6.4 TIME MANAGEMENT LESSON

In an effort to teach time management under less stressful conditions, use the teaching sequence below with tasks that are unimportant (e.g., while playing a board game, going for a walk, grocery shopping). Once the learner is doing well with nonstressful events, you can begin the process with tasks that are actually required to be completed on time.

6.4.1 Teaching Sequence

1. *Identification of elapsed time.* Start by asking the learner to note the start and end times of an activity. Then, instruct the learner to identify how long the task took to complete using the How Long Do Things Take? form (Fig. 6.4). As the learner discovers how long it takes to complete various activities, you may consider having the learner keep a list of items that take varying time lengths to complete using the Time Lengths of Activities form (Fig. 6.5).
2. *Prediction of elapsed time.* Instruct the learner to predict how long a task might take. Then, compare the learner's prediction with actual elapsed time. If the learner discovers the time length of a new activity, the learner can add this activity to the Time Lengths of Activities form (Fig. 6.5).
3. *Making and following a schedule.*
   a. *Making a practice schedule.* Choose a shortened period of the day (i.e., 2−4 hours) and work with the learner to make a schedule for that time period using the Schedule form (Fig. 6.6). Starting with a time period that includes unimportant tasks such as leisure activities with no real deadlines will make learning the basics of time management much less stressful on the learner and caregivers.

How Long Do Things Take?

Name:_____

#	Activity	Start Time	End Time	How Long?
1				
2				
3				
4				
5				
6				
7				
8				
9				
10				
11				
12				
13				
14				
15				
16				
17				
18				
19				
20				
21				
22				
23				

Figure 6.4 How Long Do Things Take? form to be used with the Time Management *lesson.*

   b. *Task analysis.* Use the Following a Schedule Task Analysis
      (Fig. 6.7) to record data on the learner's acquisition of the steps
      associated with learning to follow a schedule.
   c. *Tracking time.* Initially, it may be helpful to have the learner use
      a visual timer such as the Time Timer to keep track of the time

Time Lengths of Activities

Name: _____

#	5 minutes	10 minutes	15 minutes	20 minutes	30 minutes	45 minutes	60 minutes
1							
2							
3							
4							
5							
6							
7							
8							
9							
10							
11							
12							
13							

Figure 6.5 Time Lengths of Activities form to be used with the Time Management *lesson.*

Schedule

Name:_____   Date:_____

Start Time	Stop Time	Activity	Complete ☑

Figure 6.6 Schedule form to be used with the Time Management *lesson.*

allotted to each task. The learner should check the clock or Time Timer periodically throughout the activity to keep on schedule. If the learner is running behind and won't be able to complete the task within the remaining time allotted, ask the learner if he should speed up to finish on time or rearrange the schedule.

Following a Schedule Task Analysis

Time Frame:_____

#	Steps	Initials / Date	Initials / Date	Initials / Date	Initials / Date
1	Looks at the schedule and initiates activity, setting timer as needed.				
2	Checks remaining time during activity and determines if activity will be completed on time.				
3	If activity won't be completed on time, decides whether to speed up or continue at the same speed (knowing activity won't be completed).				
4	When time runs out, decides whether to: (1) continue activity, which involves removing or eating into time of another activity on the schedule, or (2) move on to the next activity on the schedule without finishing current activity.				
5	Places a checkmark to indicate completion.				
6	Adjusts start/stop times on schedule as needed.				
	Percentage Independent				

Figure 6.7 Following a Schedule Task Analysis to be used with the Time Management *lesson.*

    d. *Moving from practice to real schedules.* Once the learner is responding independently with a practice schedule filled with unimportant activities, teach the learner to begin making and following real schedules that pertain to activities that need to occur in daily life.

6.4.2 Mastery Criterion

1. *Identification and prediction of elapsed time.* Consider identification and prediction of elapsed time to be mastered once the learner is able to identify and predict time lengths of novel activities consistently. An example mastery criterion is performing independently in 4 out of 5 or 8 out of 10 opportunities (i.e., 80% correct).
2. *Making and following a schedule.* Consider the skill of making and following a schedule to be mastered once the learner is able to make and follow new schedules consistently. An example mastery criterion is performing the items on the Following a Schedule Task Analysis (Fig. 6.7) with 100% independence.

6.4.3 Data Collection and Graphing

1. *Identification and prediction of elapsed time.* Each time you ask the learner to identify or predict elapsed time, record whether his response is correct or whether it required a prompt. Do this across a number of opportunities and then graph the percentage correct.
2. *Making and following a schedule.* For some learners, it may be helpful to have them self-monitor their completion of steps using the task analysis. In this case, the learner will record data. However, should you choose not to use self-monitoring, the interventionist will record data. If you are using the Following a Schedule Task Analysis (Fig. 6.7), record and graph the percentage of steps the learner was able to complete independently.

6.5 PLANNING

Planning involves being able to (1) identify a goal, the steps for reaching the goal, and materials that may be needed; (2) initiate the plan; (3) monitor progress; and (4) complete the plan. At around 7 years of age, learners are able to identify a short-term goal and the steps needed to achieve it. Between 8 and 11 years, learners are able to plan simple school projects as well as how they can make and save money. They are also aware of their daily schedule and are able to keep track of their personal belongings on outings. Between 11 and 14 years, learners are able to plan and manage several long-term projects, including the timelines required for completion.

The following is a list of behaviors associated with learners who have difficulty with planning. If you are observing some of these deficits in a learner, the learner will likely benefit from activities centered on teaching planning skills:

- has difficulty figuring out how to start a task
- has difficulty completing tasks
- finds tasks with many steps difficult to do
- makes mistakes and has to redo some steps of a task in order to get it right
- does not think through the steps and materials needed to complete a task or achieve a goal

Lessons that can help teach planning skills include: (1) *Using a Planner/Device for Planning*, (2) *Planning Short-and Long-Term Goals*, and (3) *Making Social Plans and Using Social Media*.

6.6 USING A PLANNER/DEVICE FOR PLANNING

6.6.1 Prerequisite

Make sure the learner has already mastered the *Time Management* lesson in this chapter.

6.6.2 Procedure

1. *Choose a planner*. Determine with the learner what type of planner will be used (paper or electronic). If the learner has a smartphone, the calendar on the phone will be perfect for this, especially since the learner likely never goes anywhere without his phone and because the phone can provide visual and auditory reminders to the learner as needed to help keep him on schedule.
2. *Teach to use planner*. Since the learner has already acquired time management skills, focus on teaching the learner how to use the planner. For example, teach:
   a. where and how to enter activities into the schedule;
   b. how to set recurring activities, such as weekly sports practices, so that they need not be set into the calendar more than once;
   c. how to set reminders and to identify whether the reminders will be visual, auditory, or both;
   d. how to set alarms as needed.

6.7 PLANNING: SHORT- AND LONG-TERM GOALS

6.7.1 Procedure

1. *Planning worksheets*. Teach the learner to (1) identify the goal, required materials, and steps of a plan; and (2) initiate, monitor, and complete the plan using the Planning Short-Term Tasks (Fig. 6.8) and Planning Long-Term Tasks (Fig. 6.9) worksheets.
2. *Short- and long-term goals*. Examples of short-term goals that may be targeted include cleaning out the learner's desk, under the bed, dresser, closet, and bathroom cabinets/drawers. Long-term goals include school projects that are due in a couple of weeks, making the varsity basketball team, getting elected for student council treasurer, planning a party, becoming friends with a group of peers, and applying to colleges.
3. *Task analysis*. Initially, walk the learner through the steps of solving the problem using the Planning Short- and Long-Term Tasks Task Analysis (Fig. 6.10) and the questions you could ask the learner.

Planning Short-Term Tasks

Name:_____   Date:_____

Steps	Completed ☑
Goal:	

Materials Needed:

Steps	Completed ☑

My Plan (circle one): Had many problems   Had some problems   Went well   Went very well

What I would do differently next time:

Figure 6.8 Planning Short-Term Tasks Worksheet to be used with the Planning: Short- and Long-Term Goals *lesson.*

Planning Long-Term Tasks

Name:_____   Date:_____

Goal:		Due Date:
Materials Needed:		

Steps	Date I Will Complete	Completed ☑

My Plan (circle one): Had many problems   Had some problems   Went well   Went very well

What I would do differently next time:

Figure 6.9 Planning Long-Term Tasks Worksheet to be used with the Planning: Short- and Long-Term Goals *lesson.*

Planning Long-Term Goals Task Analysis

Name:_____

#	Steps	Questions (initial prompts)	Date/ Initials	Date/ Initials	Date/ Initials	Date/ Initials	Date/ Initials
1	Identifies the goal.	"What is the goal?"					
2	Identifies materials needed.	"What materials will you need?"					
3	Identifies the steps.	"What are the steps needed to meet the goal?"					
4	Schedules the steps (may use calendar/planner).	"When will you do each step?" "How much time is needed for each step?"					
5	Initiates relevant step of the plan.	"Get started."					
6	Completes the step.	"Keep going."					
7	Crosses step off or places checkmark to indicate step is complete.	"Cross the item off the list."					
8	Evaluates how the plan went (at end of plan only).	"What went well with the plan?" "What didn't go well?" "What would you do differently next time?"					
		Percentage Independent					

Figure 6.10 Planning Long-Term Goals Task Analysis to be used with the Planning: Short- and Long-Term Goals *lesson.*

4. *Prompts.*
    a. *Use shadowing.* Initially, use shadowing (see Chapter 2, Principles Behind the Lessons, for more about shadowing) to walk the learner through the steps of planning. In doing so, you can either follow the steps outlined in the Planning Short- and Long-Term Tasks Task Analysis (Fig. 6.10) and present the questions in that task analysis orally to the learner, or you can use the Planning Short-Term Tasks (Fig. 6.8) and Planning Long-Term Tasks (Fig. 6.9) worksheets, which provide written questions to which the learner should write answers (you can write them if the learner does not like to write).
    b. *Use less intrusive prompts.* Prompt correct answers to the questions using less intrusive prompts, such as leading questions, before using more intrusive prompts (see Chapter 2, Principles Behind the Lessons, for more about prompts).
    c. *Fade prompts.* If you are presenting the questions vocally to the learner, as the learner is successful, begin to fade out the use of the questions that are in the task analysis. If you are using the worksheet with the learner, fade out the use of the worksheet so that the learner can complete the steps without having to consult the worksheet. To do this, you could write the following key words on an index card: (1) Goal, (2) Materials, and (3) Steps.
5. *Task initiation.* Require the learner to continue to work on the problem until a successful solution is accomplished.

6.7.2 Mastery Criterion
Consider the skill of planning to be mastered once the learner is able to make plans for novel untrained goals consistently. An example mastery criterion could be planning to achieve three consecutive novel goals across three days independently. At that point, try to fade out the use of the task analysis and/or worksheets. However, keep in mind that some learners will not be able to engage in planning without these aides. See further ideas for fading out prompts of this type in Chapter 2, Principles Behind the Lessons.

6.7.3 Data Collection and Graphing
If you are using the Planning Short- and Long-Term Tasks Task Analysis (Fig. 6.10), graph the percentage of steps the learner was able to complete independently. If you are using either of the Planning Short-Term Tasks (Fig. 6.8) or Planning Long-Term Tasks (Fig. 6.9) worksheets, you may choose to grade them afterward for percentage of independence. In this case, you will still graph the percentage of independent steps completed.

6.8 PLANNING: SOCIAL PLANS AND SOCIAL MEDIA

6.8.1 Prerequisite

This lesson is useful for learners who have difficulty remembering to engage in behaviors that are required in order to make and maintain friendships.

6.8.2 Procedure

1. *Checklist.* Teach the learner to use the Planning Social Life Checklist (Fig. 6.11) to self-monitor her social life. The checklist is meant to include weekly goals for behaviors in which the learner plans to engage in order to make and maintain friendships. The goals should be individualized based on the learner's needs. For example, if the learner makes no effort to invite friends to do things, respond to texts, or to like friends' posts on social media, these may be goals that are chosen for the learner. Goals can also include steps to be made that week toward longer-term social goals, such as becoming friends with a particular group of peers. See the Example of Planning Social Life Checklist (Fig. 6.12) for an example of how this form is filled out.

2. *Prompts.*

   a. *Use shadowing, leading questions, and check-ins.* Initially, use shadowing to walk the learner through the steps of choosing weekly goals and making plans with friends. Use leading questions to help the learner fill out the checklist (see Chapter 2, Principles Behind the Lessons, for more about prompts). After the checklist is filled out for the week, make sure to check in with the learner on a daily basis to make sure she is still making movement toward her goals.

   b. *Fade prompts.* As the learner begins to show some independence with filling out the checklist, begin to fade out the shadowing and leading questions and only use check-ins to make sure the learner is staying on track. If the learner gets really good at responding and initiating with friends, you can start to fade out the use of the checklist so that the learner can complete the steps without having to consult the checklist. To do this, you could write key words associated with the learner's personal weekly goals on an index card. Using the goals on the Example of Planning Social Life Checklist (Fig. 6.12) as an example, you could write: (1) Texts, (2) Social media, and (3) Make plans.

Planning Social Life Checklist

Name:_____   Week of:_____

Weekly Goal	Completed ☑							Notes
	Sun	Mo	Tue	We	Thu	Fri	Sat	

Making Plans with a Friend	Completed ☑	Notes
Ask parents if it's okay for:		
Text or call to invite _____ to _____		
Plan activities with parents:		
Plan foods/drinks with parents:		
Gather materials:		

Figure 6.11 Planning Social Life Checklist to be used with the Planning: Social Plans and Social Media *lesson.*

6.8.3 Mastery Criterion

Consider the skill of planning a social life to be mastered once the learner is able to meet her goals consistently. An example mastery criterion could be engaging in social planning with 100% independence for three weeks. At that point, try to fade out the use of the

Example of Planning Social Life Checklist

Name:_____   Week of:_____

Weekly Goal	Completed ☑							Notes
	Sun	Mon	Tues	Wed	Thur	Fri	Sat	
Befriend someone on Instagram							✓	Amy
Like or comment on friends' posts 3x/wk		✓		✓			✓	Ann, Jenn, Amy
Post to Instagram 3x/wk	✓			✓		✓		
Check phone texts daily and respond	✓	✓	✓	✓	✓	✓	✓	
Send a friendly text 3 x/wk	✓		✓				✓	Tori, Jenn, Ann
Invite Tori to sleep over Friday		✓						

Making Plans with a Friend	Completed ☑	Notes
Ask parents if it's okay for: Tori to sleep over Friday	✓	Said "Yes!"
Text or call to invite Tori to sleep over	✓	Said "Yes!"
Plan activities with parents: Go to Kid's World Rent a movie	✓	iTunes
Plan foods/drinks with parents: Pizza, root beer floats, popcorn	✓	Woohoo!
Gather materials: - Going grocery shopping with Mom on Wednesday - Bring socks and tokens to Kid's World		

Figure 6.12 Example of Planning Social Life Checklist to be used with the Planning: Social Plans and Social Media *lesson.*

checklist. However, keep in mind that some learners will not be able to perform social planning without the checklist. See further ideas for fading out prompts of this type in Chapter 2, Principles Behind the Lessons.

6.8.4 Data Collection and Graphing

Grade the Planning Social Life Checklist (Fig. 6.11) at the end of the week by calculating the learner's percentage of independence. Graph percentage of independence with social planning on a weekly basis.

## CHAPTER 7

Working Memory

Working memory is the term used to refer to the ability to hold and manipulate information for short periods of time. Intelligence tests measure working memory skills by asking learners to recall digits, letters, or words forward and backward; follow multiple-step instructions; and recall information with distractors present.

Typically developing children remember and follow three-step instructions between 3 and 4 years of age. Between 5 and 8 years, they run errands involving two- to three-step directions that require moving between rooms of the house, and remember to bring paperwork to and from school. Between 8 and 11 years, they begin to run more complicated errands that require either a time delay (such as doing something after school) or moving a greater distance such as going to a neighbor's house. Additionally, they not only bring papers to and from school, but they also bring the appropriate books and assignments.

The following is a list of behaviors associated with learners who forget things. If you are observing some of these deficits in a learner, the learner will likely benefit from activities centered on improving the learner's ability to remember information:

- has difficulty completing actions that involve two or more steps
- forgets what he is doing in the middle of a task
- has difficulty completing tasks even when instructions are given
- has difficulty remembering instructions
- has difficulty remembering information

To improve the working memory skills of learners, consider working on any of the following skills:

- *Digit, letter, and word recall forward and backward.* Start with two digits and increase to four or five.

Flexible and Focused. DOI: http://dx.doi.org/10.1016/B978-0-12-809833-2.00007-8

- *Following two-, three-, and four-step instructions.* Start with related instructions such as, "Take off your shoes and put them in your closet" and move to unrelated instructions such as, "Put on your shoes, turn off the lights, get your sweatshirt, and meet me in the garage."
- *Delivering a message.* For example you might instruct, "Go tell Dad I need his help" and the learner would deliver the message to Dad.
- *Running errands.* For example, you might ask, "Can you please go get me a pencil?" or instruct, "Go to the next-door neighbors' house and ask them if they have an egg we can borrow."
- *Memory board game*
- *Online memory games*
- *Spelling words*
- *Math facts*
- *Reading comprehension*

Lessons that can be used to teach learners to remember information include: (1) *Studying Skills* (i.e., strategies for recalling information needed for tests); (2) *Remembering to Turn in Homework*; and (3) *Keeping Track of Personal Items*, such as the learner's sweatshirt, water bottle, lunch box, and cell phone.

7.1 STUDYING SKILLS

7.1.1 Corequisite

This lesson should be used in combination with the *Homework Routine* lesson in Chapter 4, Attention. In that lesson, the learner is taught to sit in a quiet location when doing homework and how to organize homework materials and complete steps. This lesson focuses on teaching various techniques for studying for tests.

7.1.2 Procedure

1. *Introduce studying strategies.* Start by teaching the learner about various studying strategies and how they can be used.
   a. *Flashcards.* These are used to memorize information such as definitions and facts for social studies, science, and reading comprehension tests. One side of the card contains a key word and the other side contains the information that needs to be memorized.

b. *Writing information multiple times.* This technique is used to memorize how to spell words for spelling tests.

c. *Rehearsing information orally.* This technique is also used to memorize how to spell words for spelling tests. Used in combination with flashcards, the learner may rehearse the information on the opposite side of the key word.

d. *Practicing.* This is used to memorize math facts or to learn how to conduct a type of math problem such as multiplying fractions or calculating the area of a shape.

e. *Mental association.* When a particular piece of information is difficult to remember, it can be helpful to teach the learner to make an association. For example, when trying to recall how to spell "dessert" versus "desert," one might think of how dessert makes you bigger so it has more than one "s."

f. *Acronyms and acrostics.* When trying to remember a list of items, the learner can make an acronym or acrostic. For example, if trying to recall all seven continents, the learner may come up with 4SEAN (for Sean) where the number 4 indicates there are four continents that start with the letter "A" and one continent that starts with each "S," "E," and "N" (South America, Europe, Antarctica, Australia, Africa, Asia, North America). A more well-known example is "Roy G. Biv" wherein the letters stand for the colors of the rainbow in the correct order (red, orange, yellow, green, blue, indigo, violet).

g. *Songs and stories.* Songs and stories can be useful for remembering information. For example, an online music video with a catchy tune called "Tour of the States" teaches the states and capitals of the United States.

h. *Visual images.* This can involve either thinking of information in pictures or using physical items to provide a visual representation. For example, months that have 31 days can be represented by each knuckle on the learner's hands, starting with labeling the pinky knuckle of the left hand "January," and then the ridge between the pinky and ring finger "February," and so on.

2. *Prompts.* When the learner is completing the homework routine and needs to study for a test, start by using shadowing. Help the learner identify an appropriate studying strategy and assist the learner to use the strategy until the learner is correctly recalling the information effortlessly. Make sure to fade prompts (see Chapter 2, Principles Behind the Lessons, for more on shadowing and prompt fading).

7.1.3 Mastery Criterion

Consider this skill mastered once the learner is able to consistently and independently identify and implement a studying strategy. An example mastery criterion is identification and implementation of a studying strategy with 80%–100% of weekly tests across two to three weeks.

7.1.4 Data Collection and Graphing

Since tests do not occur on a daily basis, it is suggested that you record and graph the percentage of weekly tests for which the learner was able to identify and implement an appropriate studying strategy.

7.2 REMEMBERING TO TURN IN HOMEWORK

7.2.1 Corequisites

Teach this lesson in conjunction with the *Organizing Homework and School Supplies* lesson in Chapter 5, Organization, and *Homework Routine* lesson in Chapter 4, Attention. If the learner has been exposed to both of these lessons, the homework should already be placed in the correct binder/location. Interestingly though, even after they have learned to be organized, some learners will forget to turn in their homework! They may have failing grades even though they have completed the work, simply because they haven't turned it in.

7.2.2 Procedure

1. *Meet with teacher(s)*. The first step to ensuring the learner is turning in homework is to have a meeting with the learner's teachers to develop a plan that everyone will be on board with for getting the homework turned in. Various ideas include:
   a. a daily verbal instruction to turn in homework made by the teacher
   b. a daily or weekly check-in at the end of class time between the learner and teacher to obtain missing homework assignments
   c. a vibrating alarm on the learner's phone to prompt turning in the homework
   d. a sign on the learner's desk that says, "Turn in homework"
2. *Prompts*. The ideas above are all prompts and some of them might be appropriate to keep in place such as the alarm and the sign; however, prompts that require the teacher to manage whether the learner turns in homework will need to be faded. It's important to look toward eventually having prompts in place that can be self-managed rather than requiring others to manage whether the learner is turning in homework.

3. *Self-evaluation.* Each time the learner receives a grade on a homework assignment, have the learner engage in self-evaluation of his performance by filling out the Self-Evaluation of Graded Assignments form (Fig. 7.1).

Self-Evaluation of Graded Assignments

Name:_____

Date: Assignment:	My Grade:
Steps	**Completed** ☑
Check each item I got wrong and figure out the correct answer.	
If I can't figure out the answer, ask for help.	
What I would do differently next time:	
Date: Assignment:	My Grade:
Steps	**Completed** ☑
Check each item I got wrong and figure out the correct answer.	
If I can't figure out the answer, ask for help.	
What I would do differently next time:	
Date: Assignment:	My Grade:
Steps	**Completed** ☑
Check each item I got wrong and figure out the correct answer.	
If I can't figure out the answer, ask for help.	
What I would do differently next time:	

Figure 7.1 Self-Evaluation of Graded Assignments form to be used with the Remembering to Turn in Homework *lesson.*

7.2.3 Mastery Criterion

Consider this skill mastered once the learner is turning in homework consistently. An example mastery criterion is turning in 90% of homework by the due date across four weeks in the absence of teacher prompts.

7.2.4 Data Collection and Graphing

Record and graph the percentage of homework assignments turned in by the due date per week.

7.3 KEEPING TRACK OF PERSONAL ITEMS

Learners with deficits in executive skills often have difficulty keeping track of their personal items. For example, they lose their cell phones, leave water bottles and jackets at school, and forget to bring home items when they go to sports practices and games or have a play-date or sleepover at a friend's house.

7.3.1 Procedure

1. *School items.* To help learners remember to bring home their jackets and water bottles when they attend school, see the School Backpack Checklist (Fig. 4.2) in Chapter 4, Attention.
2. *Extracurricular activities and outings.*
   a. *One-time activity.* Use the Packing My Bag Checklist (Fig. 7.2) to teach the learner to write down the items that are being packed as the learner is packing a bag for an outing. Have the learner place checkmarks on the checklist twice for each outing, first when packing for the outing, and again when packing to go home from the outing.
   b. *Recurring activities.* If the learner has recurring extracurricular activities, you may consider laminating a smaller version of the checklist and placing it on a key ring that attaches to the bag. This way, the learner always has access to viewing it when packing to go on and return from an outing. It might also be helpful to have specific bags that are already prepacked for particular activities so that the learner can simply check the bag before leaving the house to ensure it contains all required items.

Packing My Bag Checklist

Name:_____   Date:_____

#	Items	Packed to Take ☑	Packed to Bring Home ☑
1			
2			
3			
4			
5			
6			
7			
8			
9			
10			
11			
12			
13			
14			
15			
16			
17			
18			

Figure 7.2 Packing My Bag Checklist to be used with the Keeping Track of Personal Items *lesson.*

3. *Cell phone.*
   a. *At home.* Teach the learner to place the phone in only three possible places: (1) in her hand (when using), (2) in her pocket/purse, and (3) in one designated location in each room of the house. This practice ensures that the phone will never be left in a random unfamiliar location. Thus, when the learner cannot find her phone, she can look in all the preestablished locations, and the phone should be in one of them.
   b. *In the community.* To help ensure the learner has not left the phone somewhere when on an outing, consider placing a sign or sticker in the learner's seat of the car that reads, "Phone." The purpose of the sign is to prompt the learner to ensure she has her phone before driving away from the location. In the event that the learner leaves the phone somewhere, ensure there is a Global Positioning System tracker on the phone to make it more likely the phone will be found.

7.3.2 Mastery Criterion

Consider the skill of keeping track of personal items to be mastered once the learner avoids losing personal items consistently. An example mastery criterion is losing zero items per week for four consecutive weeks.

7.3.3 Data Collection and Graphing

Record and graph the number of items the learner loses per week.

## CHAPTER 8

Emotional Self-Regulation and Flexibility

Emotional self-regulation involves the ability to behave effectively and adaptively, even when engaged in situations that are disappointing, annoying, frustrating, stressful, anxiety-provoking, and so on. Individuals with strong emotional regulation skills are able to notice negative emotions being felt and choose to engage in behaviors that are alternatives to maladaptive behaviors like complaining, swearing, trying to escape the situation (in the case of anxiety), and raising their voice.

Strong emotional regulation skills involve taking a bird's-eye view of oneself and noticing when one is becoming emotionally charged. In that moment, emotional regulation skills consist of considering the possible consequences of one's actions and choosing to engage in coping strategies that will allow one to continue to move forward toward one's goals and values, even while feeling negative emotions. For example, when feeling angry, a learner with strong emotional regulation skills may choose to take a few deep breaths and think about how close they are to finishing a difficult task and what they will do afterward to celebrate in order to push themselves to continue to move forward with the difficult task.

The following is a list of behaviors often displayed by learners who have difficulty with self-regulation. If you are observing some of these behaviors in a learner, the learner will likely benefit from activities centered on teaching emotional self-regulation:

- tends to overreact to situations when compared to same-age peers
- remains upset about a situation for longer than same-age peers
- is short tempered and has emotional outbursts
- has mood swings
- reacts to small problems as though they are major problems

Individuals who are able to engage in emotional self-regulation are presumably much more successful in their personal and work relationships with others. The upcoming *Emotional Self-Regulation* lesson can

Flexible and Focused. DOI: http://dx.doi.org/10.1016/B978-0-12-809833-2.00008-X

be used to teach emotional coping strategies. If the learner tends to get emotionally charged due to inflexibilities, also see the *Flexibility* lesson in this chapter. Learners who perceive small problems as large problems, and thus engage in emotional outbursts when problems occur, are less likely to be able to engage in problem solving at a sufficient level. Therefore, learners with emotional self-regulation deficits may also benefit from working on the *Problem Solving* lesson in Chapter 6, Problem Solving, Time Management, and Planning, in conjunction with the upcoming *Emotional Self-Regulation* lesson. This will allow the learner to become more fluent at solving problems and better equipped to respond efficiently when problems arise. For further reading on improving emotional self-regulation, see the book, *The Incredible 5-Point Scale* by Buron and Curtis (2012).

8.1 EMOTIONAL SELF-REGULATION

8.1.1 Prerequisite
Before beginning this lesson, make sure the learner can already label emotions.

8.1.2 Procedure
1. *Wait for a good mood.* Make sure this lesson is introduced when the learner is in a good mood. Working on this lesson when the learner is already emotionally charged is not a good time to work on this lesson. Think of this lesson as a proactive approach to help the learner to identify ways to cope and manage her emotions when they arise.
2. *Emotional levels chart.* Start by creating a visual aid with the learner that includes several emotional levels, beginning with a "feeling good" face and moving in the direction of a feeling frustrated and/or angry face (see Emotional Levels Chart, Fig. 8.1). Allow the learner to come up with her own labels for the various levels, and write them in underneath the faces. One example is: (1) Feeling Good, (2) A Little Upset, (3) Upset, and (4) Very Upset.
3. *Teaching sequence.*
   a. *Teach to relate emotional levels to situations.* You can do this by (1) asking the learner to identify situations that make her feel each emotional level, and (2) presenting scenarios and asking the learner to identify the emotional level that she usually feels in such situations. Fill in the answers to these questions in the blank column to the right on the Emotional Levels Chart

Emotional Levels Chart

Figure 8.1 Emotional Levels Chart to be used with the Emotional Self-Regulation *lesson.*

(Fig. 8.1). This is also a good time to talk to the learner about what the appropriate reactions should be to various scenarios. For example, some situations that really stress out the learner can be brushed off and labeled no big deal, whereas others might be considered a big deal. Teach the learner to identify whether various situations should be treated as a big deal or no big deal.

b. *Teach coping strategies.* These are strategies that can be used when the learner is feeling emotionally charged. Have the learner actually practice each of the strategies and identify ones she thinks will be helpful. Give the learner hypothetical situations that could occur, and instruct the learner to role-play how she can use a coping strategy. Examples of coping strategies include:

    i. taking deep breaths
    ii. making positive statements ("I am okay. I can deal with this.")
    iii. counting to 20
    iv. asking for a break
    v. asking for help
    vi. writing in a journal
    vii. talking to a safe person/friend
    viii. thinking of a compromise
    ix. coming up with a different idea or plan
    x. thinking about something that makes the learner happy
    xi. letting it go
    xii. going for a walk or exercising

c. *Contrive opportunities to practice.* Next, explain to the learner that in order to avoid getting to a level three or four on the emotional scale, it would be helpful for her to start using coping strategies once her emotions reach level two. Once the learner has identified coping strategies that she thinks will be helpful, tell the learner that a difficult situation is going to happen in a given setting and instruct her to decide in advance how she will remain calm. Then, contrive or capture the difficult situation in the planned setting, and help the learner to use the coping strategy.

d. *Capture opportunities to practice in the natural environment.* Once the learner is able to calm down when warned in advance that a difficult situation is going to occur, begin to ask the learner what she will do in a real-life upcoming situation if it becomes difficult. At this point, you are no longer stating that a difficult situation will absolutely occur but that the learner should be prepared at all times for the possibility. In this case, the learner will be expected to use coping strategies as needed when difficult situations arise in the natural environment.

4. *Plan in advance*. If the learner has recurring situations that tend to make her emotionally charged, have the learner identify how she will cope with that situation every time it arises. You can even have the learner write the plan for what she will do at each emotional level on the Emotional Levels Chart (Fig. 8.1).
5. *Include effective behavioral intervention strategies*. This lesson teaches the learner to engage in the verbal and cognitive skills necessary to begin to plan and control her own behavior when she is experiencing negative emotions. Another way to think about this lesson is that it teaches the learner to choose behaviors that have more beneficial outcomes (e.g., avoiding getting in trouble, making friends, etc.) and to avoid behaviors that will have more negative consequences (e.g., punishment from teacher, avoidance by peers, etc.). Although learning this verbal/cognitive skill will be helpful, it is not a replacement for meaningful consequences for the learner's behavior. For example, when the learner breathes deeply and does not have a tantrum, she should gain access to a reinforcer; whereas, when the learner has a tantrum, she should not get what she wants.

8.1.3 Mastery Criterion
Mastery will occur at each phase of the teaching sequence outlined. Here are some sample mastery criteria that you can use for each phase of the teaching sequence.

1. 80–100% correct identification of situations that make the learner feel each emotional level across two to three consecutive sessions
2. 80–100% correct identification of the emotional level felt in various situations across two to three consecutive sessions
3. 80–100% correct identification of situations that are considered a big deal versus no big deal across two to three consecutive sessions
4. 80–100% correct role-play of each coping strategy across two to three consecutive sessions
5. 80–100% independent implementation of a coping strategy when prewarned that a difficult situation is going to occur across five consecutive situations
6. 80–100% independent implementation of a coping strategy when *not* prewarned that a difficult situation is going to occur across five consecutive situations

8.1.4 Data Collection and Graphing

Collect data on correct versus prompted responses and convert to and graph percentage correct across sessions.

8.2 FLEXIBILITY

Flexibility involves the willingness to adapt to one's environment by engaging in different behaviors when things in one's environment change. Typically developing toddlers can get used to routines and engage in tantrums when schedules or routines change. However, between 5 and 7 years of age, children generally become more accepting of reasonable routine changes. For some children with autism spectrum disorder, variability, per se, seems to be aversive and anxiety-provoking. Inflexibilities can include anything from not wanting an item to move from its normal position in the home, to insisting on particular sequences of activities, to always taking the same routes on outings, to being inflexible when plans don't turn out as expected.

The following is a list of behaviors often displayed by learners who have difficulty with flexibility. If you are observing some of these behaviors in a learner, the learner will likely benefit from activities centered on teaching flexible behavior:

- does not react well to a change in plans or routines
- does not react well or takes a while to warm up to new situations
- wants things done in a specific way and becomes upset if they are changed
- perseverates on topics and activities
- has difficulty interacting in unfamiliar social situations
- does not want to try new things
- has particularly limited varieties in food or toy preferences
- dictates to others how they are "supposed" to do things

See the upcoming *Flexibility* lesson for specific tips for teaching learners to be more flexible. If the learner tends to have difficulty managing emotional reactions to inflexibilities, it will be helpful to work on the *Emotional Self-Regulation* lesson (also in this chapter) in combination with this lesson. For further reading on improving flexibility, see the book, *Unstuck and On Target! An Executive*

Function Curriculum to Improve Flexibility for Children With Autism Spectrum Disorders (Cannon, Kenworthy, Alexander, Werner, & Anthony, 2011).

8.3 FLEXIBILITY LESSON

8.3.1 Procedure

1. Start by making a list of situations in which the learner is inflexible. Some of these situations you will use to directly teach the learner to be more flexible and some you will save to test for generalization later. Examples include:
   a. being barefoot
   b. crinkled rug
   c. someone coming over when unexpected
   d. driving or walking using a different route
   e. plans changing
   f. items moving to a new location
   g. lit candles
   h. touching sand
2. *Exposure and response prevention.*
   a. *Expose.* Expose the learner to the situation in which he is usually inflexible and prevent the learner from being able to "fix" the situation or escape it. For example, if the learner screams every time the strings on the rug are crinkled, tell the learner that you are going to crinkle the rug strings, and he is not allowed to fix it by straightening the strings.
   b. *Reinforce.* Provide a reinforcer for calmly tolerating the situation. At first, you may need to use a very strong reinforcer for a very small amount of calm tolerance. For example, if the learner remains calm while you sing a song using the incorrect lyrics for 5 seconds, you might give him 2 minutes access to his favorite video on a computer.
   c. *Repeat with other inflexibilities.* Continue this process with all other inflexible situations that matter to the learner's parents. It's important to include the learner's parents or other caregivers in the decision of what inflexible situations will be targeted. For example, they might not care if their child ever goes to the beach and therefore tolerating sand may not be relevant to them. However, if they live near the beach and wish they could go all the time, this might be important to them.

d. *Take baby steps.* Start small to help the learner be successful. Start with inflexible situations that are not the most difficult ones for the learner so the learner can contact reinforcement easily for remaining calm. For example, you might start by singing the song "Happy Birthday" without saying the word "birthday."

e. *Test for generalization.* Continue teaching new situations until the learner calmly tolerates situations you have never addressed.

3. *Teach definition of flexibility.* You can also teach the learner the vocabulary words "flexible" and "rigid" and what it means to be flexible and rigid. Explain that objects can be flexible, e.g., objects that bend (e.g., cooked noodles, rubber bands, clay, flowers) are flexible and objects that are stiff (e.g., marker, remote control, monkey bar, bouncy ball) are rigid. Things that are flexible change, they are bendable, and they are not always the same; whereas, things that are rigid do not change, are not bendable, and are always the same.

4. *Teach thinking flexibly.* Then, explain that our minds can also be flexible or rigid. When we are willing to let someone change our minds about something, when we decide to try something a new way or when we do something different from usual, we are having a flexible or open mind. Further, explain that when we are willing to be flexible, we don't have to get upset as easily when things don't go as planned, because we are open to doing things differently. When we are rigid, we have no choice but to get upset because we are stuck in our thinking. Thus, flexibility gives us the freedom to choose to do something differently instead of being stuck and mad about it.

5. *Use flexibility worksheet.* Give the learner some scenarios to work through and have the learner think about what would happen if he were rigid versus flexible. See Table 8.1 for sample scenarios. Use the Flexibility Worksheet (Fig. 8.2) to write out with the learner what would happen if he were rigid versus inflexible. This worksheet also teaches the learner to identify what he will do to remain flexible. Some options include:

a. *Let it be.* This option involves simply refraining from trying to fix or escape the situation. For example, if the learner gets upset when the rug strings are crinkled, he will choose to let them be crinkled rather than trying to fix them. If the learner has a tantrum when he touches sand, he will tolerate touching sand. It's fine to start small and use desensitization by having the learner

Table 8.1 Examples of Rigid Versus Flexible Behavior in Situations		
Situations	**Rigid**	**Flexible**
Mom drives a different route	Scream and cry; make mom upset with me	Let it be; take deep breaths; I can still get there
Change in schedule/routine	Refuse to participate; running late	Let it be; think of happy place; find another time to do the thing I wanted to do
How a game is played	Refuse to play the game; play alone	Compromise; get to use some of each of our ideas for rules
Friend wants to play a different game	Act mad; refuse to have fun	Compromise; get to play a little of both games; flip a coin to see whose game goes first
Lost a piece of a game	Refuse to play the game; have nothing to do; friends don't want to play with me	Back-up plan; use a piece from another game; still get to play and have fun
Forgot favorite sweater	Have to go home; refuse to participate	Back-up plan; borrow a sweater
Substitute teacher	Refuse to stay at school; have a tantrum in class	Back-up plan; get a moment to calm down in another room, and then go back to class
Friend comes over unexpectedly when about to leave to do something fun	Yell at friend for coming and send them away	Back-up plan; ask friend to join in what was planned for that afternoon

first look at sand, then touch with a finger, then hold sand in hand, then pick up and pour sand with hands, then help build a sand castle, and so on.

b. *Back-up plan.* Explain to the learner that when he has high or specific expectations about how something is going to turn out, there is always the chance of being disappointed. Discuss with the learner how having specific expectations is rigid thinking and can lead to disappointment. Explain that often things do not turn out as expected, thus it's helpful to have an open mind and avoid having specific expectations that may not come to fruition. For example, if the learner was supposed to have a play-date at his friend's house and was anticipating all the fun games that they would play at the friend's house, but their mothers decide instead to take the boys to the park, the learner's rigid thinking about the plan will lead to major disappointment and frustration. Using this type of example, teach the learner that when our plans don't work out, we need a back-up plan. Explain to the learner that if he remains rigid about the plan, he will not be able to have fun. However, if he comes up with a back-up plan

Flexibility Worksheet

Inflexible Situation:	
What will happen if I'm rigid:	**What will happen if I'm flexible:**
How I will be flexible: Let it be Compromise Back-Up Plan	Other: _____
Coping strategy I will use:	

Figure 8.2 Flexibility Worksheet to be used with the Flexibility *lesson.*

about what they can do at the park or when he can go to the friend's house on another day soon, he can still have fun. Start small and don't just talk about it; role-play it with the learner and practice across many different examples.

c. *Compromise* Sometimes the learner and a second person will not agree on what they want to do. For example, during a play-date, the learner may want to play video games but the peer may want to play a board game. If the learner is rigid in his thinking, he will not be able to have a good time with the peer because he will be stuck on the idea of playing video games. Teach the learner that he and the peer can choose to compromise so that they each get to do what they want. In this case, the learner and peer could play both video *and* board games. To determine which activity will be done first, they could flip a coin, choose a number between 1 and 10, or play the rock, paper, scissors game. The winner would get to choose the first activity.

8.3.2 Mastery Criterion

Consider flexibility to be mastered once the learner is able to be flexible across novel untrained situations consistently. An example mastery criterion is a decrease of at least 90% in rates of inflexible behavior across observation sessions for two to three weeks across various inflexibilities.

8.3.3 Data Collection and Graphing

During the exposure and response prevention procedure, you could collect data on frequency of behaviors that indicate inflexibility. This will vary for each learner but could be anything such as whining, crying, screaming, throwing self on the floor, trying to fix the situation, and so forth. Then, convert the frequency to rate per minute by dividing the total frequency by the number of minutes of the observation. Graph the rate of inflexible behaviors per minute each session.

## CHAPTER 9

Troubleshooting

The skills you are going to teach with this manual are highly complex, much more complex than those traditionally taught in applied behavior analysis programs. Indeed, many typically developing children and adults could use help in most of these skills! Therefore, do not be surprised if you find teaching these skills more difficult than teaching simpler skills. Still, if you know how to use evidence-based behavioral teaching procedures, follow the steps in this book carefully, and thoughtfully customize them to the needs of your unique learner, acquisition of skills will occur. If you are not noticing improvements, there are a variety of things to consider. This chapter briefly reviews some of the more important troubleshooting tips that will be useful in teaching executive function skills.

9.1 ANTECEDENT MANIPULATIONS

Include preferred tasks. When possible, choose tasks that are similar to preferred activities that the learner has no problem carrying out. For example, when working on increasing sustained attention, you could initially choose tasks that are similar to those to which the learner can already sustain attention. Then, as the learner is successful with those types of tasks, you could gradually branch out to tasks that are less preferred.

Write for the learner initially. This manual comes with many forms to be filled out. Some are intended for the learner to fill out. If the learner does not like to write, you can adapt the lessons by having the learner state the information while you write it. You may want to consider a separate goal for increasing the learner's tolerance for writing, as this will be helpful across most executive function lessons.

Flexible and Focused. DOI: http://dx.doi.org/10.1016/B978-0-12-809833-2.00009-1

9.2 REINFORCEMENT PROCEDURES

Make reinforcers contingent. Avoid allowing learners to have free access to highly preferred items that will be used as reinforcers. Providing free access will lessen the value of the reinforcer and the learner will be unmotivated to work to earn the items. Additionally, since electronics are a huge source of reinforcement for learners these days, it is recommended that you avoid allowing the learner to have free access to electronics and other highly preferred items. If you or the learner's caregivers are hesitant to restrict access to electronics too much, you can consider reserving a particular video game so that it can only be accessed when responding correctly during executive function training.

Increase quantity or quality of reinforcers. Try providing more frequent or higher-quality reinforcers. For example, instead of points, you might need to provide a break with a reinforcer after each response or task is completed or after a specified amount of elapsed time working on a task.

Thin schedule gradually. If newly acquired skills do not maintain, you may have thinned the reinforcement schedule too quickly. In this case, make sure there are natural reinforcers and perhaps additional programmed reinforcers in place. Beware that removing reinforcement too quickly can result in the newly learned behavior decreasing and ultimately ceasing to occur. The goal is for naturally occurring reinforcers to eventually come to maintain responding; however, for some learners, there are no naturally occurring reinforcers. Naturally occurring reinforcers tend to be things like attention and recognition, getting a good grade, avoiding failure, feeling good about oneself, and so on. Some learners are not motivated by these types of consequences, thus such consequences do not serve as reinforcers. These learners will continue to need some sort of programmed reinforcers from caregivers, whether that is an allowance or access to preferred items.

9.3 SUFFICIENT LEARNING OPPORTUNITIES

The natural consequences of poor executive function skills can be large but not frequent enough to learn from. Therefore, it is important to make sure that there are frequent learning opportunities when teaching executive function skills. Like any other skills, practice makes perfect. It is recommended that you choose only one or two behaviors to focus on at a time so that you can put the amount of energy required into teaching those skills to mastery. The more behaviors you choose to tackle at once, the more stressful the experience will be both for the learner and the caregivers. Once you've chosen the target behaviors, contrive and capture opportunities to practice them often. Always be on the lookout for how you can contrive a larger number of practice opportunities. For example, if you have 30 minutes to work on problem solving, consider solving three smaller problems that will require about 10 minutes each, rather than one larger problem that will require all 30 minutes.

9.4 COMPONENT SKILLS AND PREREQUISITE SKILLS

If a learner is having difficulty making progress with one of the lessons in this book, consider breaking the skill you are currently working on into smaller component skills and teaching each skill one at a time. In addition, watch out for prerequisite skills that might not be strong enough. For example, problem solving and emotional self-regulation require the learner to talk to himself about potential future behaviors and what outcomes they might produce. If the learner does not already have the ability to talk about immediately present current behaviors and the outcomes they produce (talking about cause-and-effect relations between behaviors and consequences, a.k.a. rule-deriving), then he may need to be taught this skill separately first.

9.5 ATTENTION DEFICITS

If the learner feels overwhelmed or unable to attend to a task from start to finish, try using a forward or backward chaining procedure as described in Chapter 2, Principles Behind the Lessons. You may also consider dividing a task (e.g., homework routine) into smaller sitting intervals. See the *Sustained Attention* lesson in Chapter 4, Attention, for more details about how to increase the learner's capacity to sustain attention to tasks.

9.6 APPS

While this manual provides paper/pencil tools to teach executive function skills, a large variety of electronic apps are commercially available. If you think the learner may respond better to technology than the paper/pencil methods provided in this manual, you might want to search for applications that can complement or support the strategies in this manual.

9.7 MAKE IT FUN

Executive function skills can be frustrating for learners who do not already have them and they can be confusing and daunting for practitioners to teach. Make sure to build fun into your teaching strategies whenever possible. Lessons can be made into games, the learner's favorite characters or movies can be incorporated into lessons, and so on. A good sign that you are succeeding in making it fun is that you and the learner are both smiling. Keep it upbeat and remember that the ultimate smile for you is going to come when you see your learner achieve a whole new level of independence and self-determination!

ADDITIONAL RESOURCES

Baltruschat, L., Hasselhorn, M., Tarbox, J., Dixon, D. R., Najdowski, A. C., Mullins, R. D., et al. (2011a). Addressing working memory in children with autism through behavioral intervention. *Research in Autism Spectrum Disorders*, 5(1), 267–276.

Baltruschat, L., Hasselhorn, M., Tarbox, J., Dixon, D. R., Najdowski, A. C., Mullins, R. D., et al. (2011b). Further analysis of the effects of positive reinforcement on working memory in children with autism. *Research in Autism Spectrum Disorders*, 5(2), 855–863.

Baltruschat, L., Hasselhorn, M., Tarbox, J., Dixon, D. R., Najdowski, A., Mullins, R. D., et al. (2012). The effects of multiple exemplar training on a working memory task involving sequential responding in children with autism. *The Psychological Record*, 62(3), 549.

Buron, K. D., & Curtis, M. (2012). *The incredible 5-point scale: The significantly improved and expanded second edition.* Shawnee Mission, KS: AAPC Publishing.

Cannon, L., Kenworthy, L., Alexander, K. C., Werner, M. A., & Anthony, L. (2011). *Unstuck and on target! An executive function curriculum to improve flexibility for children with autism spectrum disorders.* Baltimore, MD: Paul H. Brookes Publishing Company.

Dawson, P., & Guare, R. (2009). *Smart but scattered: The revolutionary "executive skills" approach to helping kids reach their potential.* New York, NY: The Guilford Press.

Dawson, P., & Guare, R. (2010). *Executive skills in children and adolescents: A practical guide to assessment and intervention* (2nd ed.). New York, NY: The Guilford Press.

Hayes, S. C., Gifford, E. V., & Ruckstuhl, L. E., Jr. (1996). Relational frame theory and executive function: A behavioral approach. In G. R. Lyon, & N. A. Krasnegor (Eds.), *Attention, memory, and executive function* (pp. 279–306). Baltimore, MD: Brookes Publishing.

Najdowski, A. C., Persicke, A., & Kung, E. (2014). Executive functions. In D. Granpeesheh, J. Tarbox, A. Najdowski, & J. Kornack (Eds.), *Evidence-based intervention for children with autism: The CARD model* (pp. 353–385). New York, NY: Elsevier.

Persicke, A., Clair, M. S., Tarbox, J., Najdowski, A., Ranick, J., Yu, Y., et al. (2013). Teaching children with autism to attend to socially relevant stimuli. *Research in autism spectrum disorders*, 7(12), 1551–1557.

Rehfeldt, R. A., & Barnes-Holmes, Y. (Eds.), (2009). *Derived relational responding: Applications for learners with autism and other developmental disabilities: A progressive guide to change* Oakland, CA: New Harbinger.

Stewart, I., Roche, B. T., O'Hora, D., & Tarbox, J. (2013). *Education, intellectual development, and relational frame theory. Advances in relational frame theory & contextual behavioral science: Research & application.* Oakland, CA: New Harbinger.

Tarbox, J., & Najdowski, A. C. (2014). Teaching cognitive skills to children with autism. In J. Tarbox, D. Dixon, P. Sturmey, & J. Matson (Eds.), *Handbook of early intervention for autism spectrum disorders: Research, policy, and practice.* New York, NY: Springer.

Tarbox, J., & Persicke, A. (2014). *Treatment of working memory in autism. Comprehensive guide to autism* (pp. 2159–2171). New York, NY: Springer.

REFERENCES

Buron, K. D., & Curtis, M. (2012). *The incredible 5-point scale: The significantly improved and expanded second edition*. Shawnee Mission, KS: AAPC Publishing.

Cannon, L., Kenworthy, L., Alexander, K. C., Werner, M. A., & Anthony, L. (2011). *Unstuck and on target! An executive function curriculum to improve flexibility for children with autism spectrum disorders*. Baltimore, MD: Paul H. Brookes Publishing Company.

Gioia, G. A., Isquith, P. K., Guy, S. C., & Kenworthy, L. (2000). *Behavior Rating Inventory of Executive Function: BRIEF*. Odessa, FL: Psychological Assessment Resources.

Maurice, C. E., Green, G. E., & Luce, S. C. (1996). *Behavioral intervention for young children with autism: A manual for parents and professionals*. Austin, TX: Pro-Ed.

Skinner, B. F. (1974). *About behaviorism*. New York, NY: Random House, Inc.

Note: Page numbers followed by "*f*" and "*t*" refer to figures and tables, respectively.

A

Acronyms and acrostics, 83
Antecedent manipulations, 101
Applied behavior analysis (ABA), 4, 10, 19
Apps, 103–104
Attention deficits, 103
Attention skills, 31
  homework routine, 36–42
    data collection and graphing, 41–42
    homework planning sheet, 39–41
    long-term school projects, 42
    mastery criterion, 41
    prerequisites, 36
    procedure, 37–39
  morning and evening routines, 34–36
    data collection and graphing, 36
    mastery criterion, 36
    prerequisites, 34
    procedure, 34–35
  sustained attention, 42–45
    data collection and graphing, 42
    mastery criterion, 44–45
    prerequisites, 42–44
    troubleshooting, 45
Autism spectrum disorder (ASD), 4–5, 94

B

Backpack, organizational scheme for, 51
Backpack checklist, 37, 37*f*
Back-up plan, 97–99
Backward chaining, 15–16
Board certified behavior
    analysts (BCBAs), 5

C

Caregivers, training, 19
Chaining, 15–17
  procedures, 15–16
    backward chaining, 15–16
    choice of, 16–17
    forward chaining, 15
    total task chaining, 16
Circuit training exercise apps, 12
Cleaning bedroom, 48–50
  data collection and graphing, 50
  mastery criterion, 49
  procedure, 48
Cleaning Bedroom Task Analysis, 49*f*, 50
Component skills and prerequisite skills, 103
Coping strategies, teaching, 92
Countdown beeping timers, 11
Countdown visual timers, 12

D

Data collection and graphing, 20, 26–27
  cleaning bedroom, 50
  emotional self-regulation, 94
  flexibility, 99
  homework assignments, 86
  homework routine, 41–42
  keeping track of personal items, 88
  morning and evening routines, 36
  organizing personal spaces, 55
  problem solving, 63
  short- and long-term goals, 75
  social plans and social media, 79
  studying skills, 84
  time management, 70
Disengagement, 33
Disorganized children, 2–3
Divided attention, 33

E

Elapsed time, identification and prediction of,
    65, 69–70
Emotional Levels Chart, 90, 91*f*
Emotional self-regulation, 89–94
  data collection and graphing, 94
  effective behavioral intervention strategies,
    inclusion of, 93
  Emotional Levels Chart, 90, 91*f*
  mastery criterion, 93
  planning in advance, 93
  prerequisite, 90
  procedure, 90–93
  teaching sequence, 90–92
    capturing opportunities to practice in
      natural environment, 92

Emotional self-regulation (*Continued*)
   contrive opportunities to practice, 92
   coping strategies, 92
   teaching to relate emotional levels to
     situations, 90–91
   waiting for good mood, 90
Executive function, 1, 3
   deficits, 4
   skills, 104
Experiential prompt, 13
Extracurricular activities and
   outings, 86–87

F
Fade prompts, 16, 63, 75–76
Flashcards, 82
Flexibility, 94–99
   back-up plan, 97–99
   data collection and graphing, 99
   defining, 96
   exposure and response prevention, 92
   Flexibility Worksheet, 96–99, 98*f*
   mastery criterion, 99
   procedure, 95–99
   rigid versus flexible behavior in
     situations, 97*t*
Forward chaining, 15
Free access, avoiding, 101–102
Fun, making, 104

G
Generalization, 17–18, 96
Global Positioning System tracker, 88
Goal setting, 27
Goal-directed behavior, 1

H
Home desk, 51
Homework and school supplies, organizing,
   50–51
   backpack, 51
   desk, 51
   schoolwork, 50–51
Homework routine, 36–42
   data collection and graphing, 41–42
   homework planning sheet, 39–41, 40*f*
   long-term school projects, 42
   mastery criterion, 41
   prerequisites, 36
   procedure, 37–39
   task analysis, 37–38, 39*f*

I
Inhibitory control, 23
Intelligence tests, 81
Intermittent reinforcement, 8–9
Interval beeping apps, 12

L
Leading questions, 12–13, 76
Learning opportunities, 102–103
Less intrusive prompts, 61–62, 75
Long-term school projects, 42

M
Maintenance, 18–20
   self-monitoring, 19–20
   thinning reinforcement, 19
   training caregivers in, 19
Mastery criterion, 28
   cleaning bedroom, 49
   emotional self-regulation, 93
   flexibility, 99
   homework routine, 41
   keeping track of personal items, 88
   morning and evening routines, 36
   organizing personal spaces, 54–55
   problem solving, 63
   remembering to turn in homework, 86
   short- and long-term goals, 75
   social plans and social media, 77–78
   studying skills, 84
   sustained attention, 44–45
   time management, 69
Morning and evening routines, 34–36
   checklist, 35*f*
   data collection and graphing, 36
   mastery criterion, 36
   prerequisites, 34
   procedure, 34–35
Multiple exemplar, 17–18

N
Naturally occurring reinforcers, 102
Nonsocial problems, 57–58, 59*t*

O
Organization, 47
   cleaning bedroom, 48–50
     data collection and graphing, 50
     mastery criterion, 49
     procedure, 48
   homework and school supplies, organizing,
     50–51

backpack, 51
desk, 51
schoolwork, 50–51
personal spaces, organizing, 51–55
data collection and graphing, 55
mastery criterion, 54–55
procedure, 51–54
troubleshooting, 55

P

Pair reinforcement with praise, 9
Personal spaces, organizing, 51–55
data collection and graphing, 55
mastery criterion, 54–55
procedure, 51–54
troubleshooting, 55
Planning, 70
planner/device for, 71
prerequisite, 71
procedure, 71
short- and long-term goals, 71–75
data collection and graphing, 75
mastery criterion, 75
procedure, 71–75
social plans and social media, 76–79
data collection and graphing, 79
mastery criterion, 77–78
prerequisite, 76
procedure, 76
Positive reinforcement, 7–10
effectiveness of reinforcers, 9–10
pair reinforcement with praise, 9
reinforcers varying across individuals, 9
Practice schedule, making, 65
Prerequisite skills, 103
Problem solving, 57–58
data collection and graphing, 63
and flexibility, 1–2
mastery criterion, 63
procedure, 58–63
troubleshooting, 63–64
Problem Solving Worksheets, 61f, 62f
Problem-Solving Task Analysis, 60f
Prompt fading, 14
Prompting, types of, 10–14
devices, 11–12
countdown beeping timers, 11
countdown visual timers, 12
interval beeping apps, 12
experiential prompt, 13
leading questions, 12–13
shadowing, 11
visual aids, 13–14

R

Recall, 12, 81, 83
Reinforcement, 9–10, 15–16, 39, 44, 48
positive, 7–10
procedures, 101–102
thinning, 19
Reinforcers, 101–102
effectiveness of, 9–10
identifying, 27
increase quantity or quality of, 102
tangible, 7–8
varying across individuals, 9

S

Saliency, determining, 33
Schedule, making and following, 69–70
Scheduling activities, 64
School desk, organizational scheme for, 51
Schoolwork, organizational scheme for, 50–51
Self-awareness, 23–26
procedure, 24–26
Self-Awareness Worksheet, 24, 25f, 26
Self-evaluation, 85, 85f
teaching, 28
Self-management, 2–3, 14, 23, 26–29
prerequisite, 26
procedure, 26–29
data collection, 26–27
duration, 27
goal setting, 27
identifying target behavior, 26
making new goals and a terminal goal, 28
reinforce, identifying, 27
self-evaluation, teaching, 28
self-monitoring, teaching, 28
Self-monitoring
maintenance, 19–20
teaching, 28
Self-regulation, emotional. *See* Emotional
self-regulation
Shadowing, 11, 58–60
short- and long-term goals, 75
Short- and long-term goals, 71–75
data collection and graphing, 75
mastery criterion, 75
procedure, 71–75
Social plans and social media, 76–79
checklist, 76, 77f, 78f
data collection and graphing, 79
mastery criterion, 77–78
prerequisite, 76
procedure, 76
Social problems, 57–58, 59t

Songs and stories, 83
Stimulus orienting, 32
Studying skills, 82–84
    corequisite, 82
    data collection and graphing, 84
    mastery criterion, 84
    procedure, 82–83
Sustained attention, 1–2, 42–45
    data collection and graphing, 42
    mastery criterion, 44–45
    prerequisites, 42–44
    troubleshooting, 45

T
Target behavior, 28, 42
    identifying, 26
Task analysis, 15, 66, 71–74
    homework routine, 37–38, 39f
Task initiation, 1–2
Tasks, preferred, 101
Teachers, meeting with, 84
Teaching skills, 7–8, 18
Time management, 1–2, 17, 64–70
    data collection and graphing, 70
    mastery criterion, 69
    teaching sequence, 65–69
Total task chaining, 16–17
Tracking time, 66–68
Troubleshooting, 45, 55, 63–64, 101
    antecedent manipulations, 101

apps, 103–104
attention deficits, 103
component skills and prerequisite
    skills, 103
reinforcement procedures, 101–102
sufficient learning opportunities, 102–103
sustained attention, 45

V
Visual aids, 6, 13–14, 51
Visual images, 83

W
Working memory, 1–2, 81
    keeping track of personal items, 86–88
        data collection and graphing, 88
        mastery criterion, 88
        procedure, 86–88
    remembering to turn in homework,
        84–86
        corequisites, 84
        data collection and graphing, 86
        mastery criterion, 86
        procedure, 84–85
    studying skills, 82–84
        corequisite, 82
        data collection and graphing, 84
        mastery criterion, 84
        procedure, 82–83